THE RHINOCEROS

Look for these and other books in the
Lucent Endangered Animals and Habitats series:

The Elephant
The Giant Panda
The Oceans
The Rhinoceros
The Shark
The Whale
The Wolf

Other related titles in the Lucent Overview series:

Acid Rain
Endangered Species
Energy Alternatives
Environmental Groups
Garbage
The Greenhouse Effect
Ocean Pollution
Oil Spills
Ozone
Pesticides
Population
Rainforests
Recycling
Vanishing Wetlands
Zoos

THE RHINOCEROS

BY MARY HULL

Endangered
Animals &
Habitats

LUCENT BOOKS, INC.
SAN DIEGO, CALIFORNIA

LUCENT *Overview Series*

Library of Congress Cataloging-in-Publication Data

Hull, Mary.
   The rhinoceros / by Mary Hull.
       p.   cm. — (Endangered animals & habitats) (Lucent
   overview series)
   Includes bibliographical references (p.   ) and index.
   Summary: Presents an overview of various species of rhino-
   ceroses, how they have become endangered, and what is being
   done to protect them from extinction.
   ISBN 1-56006-461-7 (lib. bdg. : alk. paper)
   1. Rhinoceroses—Juvenile literature.   2. Endangered species—
   Juvenile literature.   [1. Rhinoceroses.   2. Endangered species.]
   I. Title.   II. Series.   III. Series: Lucent overview series.
   QL737.U63H85   1998
   599.66'8—dc21   97-46766
                                                          CIP
                                                           AC

Copyright © 1998 by Lucent Books, Inc.
P.O. Box 289011, San Diego, CA 92198-9011
Printed in the U.S.A.

Contents

Introduction

Rhinos have lived on the earth for 40 million years. As recently as 1900 there were approximately 1 million rhinos across Asia and Africa, but their numbers have since plummeted. Today all five species of rhinoceros are listed as endangered under the United States Endangered Species Act of 1973, which was signed into law for the purpose of preserving biodiversity. It is estimated that fewer than eleven thousand rhinos exist in the wild; Javan rhinos, the rarest species, number fewer than one hundred animals. Rhinos are one of the twelve most threatened animals on Earth, and their only natural predator is the species *Homo sapiens*—humans. Although the rhinoceros is protected by an international treaty known as the Convention on International Trade in Endangered Species (CITES), created in 1977 and signed by over 130 countries, rhino populations continue to decline.

By learning more about rhinos, such as where and how they live, how they reproduce, and what they eat, people may be able to better help them and protect the habitats where they live.

A threefold threat

Endangered is a term applied to both animals and plants, as well as to habitats—physical environments where species live and interact. A species cannot survive without a supporting environment, so habitat destruction leads to animal and plant extinction. While the extinction of species is part of the natural process of evolution, the rate of extinction depends on many factors humans can control. To-day human activities are changing the complex mix of organisms and environments, called ecosystems, faster than animal and plant species can adapt, and the number of endangered species and habitats grows.

Scientists have identified three major causes of endangerment and extinction: loss of habitat, introduced species, and overexploitation. Loss of habitat, usually through the encroachment of human beings, is currently considered the greatest cause of species extinction. Introduced species, whether brought to a new setting accidentally or intentionally, can change the ecology of a region, edging out certain species that had previously thrived. Overexploitation occurs when a species considered a resource is "consumed" faster than it can reproduce. The rhinoceros faces all three of these threats to survival. Its range in Asia and Africa has shrunk as humans have targeted more land for residential and commercial development. Now largely restricted to game parks and reserves, rhinos occupy a tiny fraction of their former habitat. Humans are the introduced species that is edging out the rhinoceros. Rhinos are also

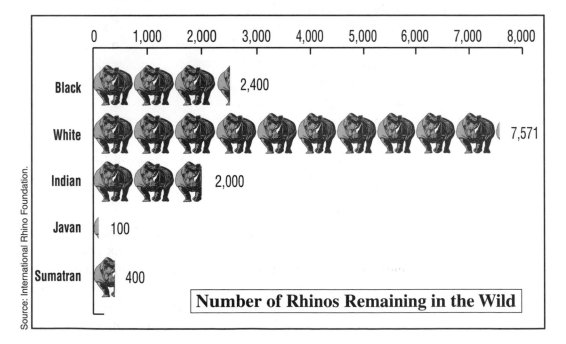

Source: International Rhino Foundation.

Number of Rhinos Remaining in the Wild

overexploited; they have been hunted throughout history for their horns and body parts, which are used in many traditional Asian medicines. The steady demand for these products has fueled a serious poaching problem that has decimated rhino populations and further limited supply, particularly in Asia.

Rhino conservation is a complex issue, pitting legitimate human needs against the animal's requirements and competing strategies against one another. Various local and international efforts range from protecting rhinos in their habitat to going after the consumers of rhino products. By educating people about the rhinoceros, increasing public awareness of its endangerment, and discussing the costs of the effort, conservationists hope to save this rugged-looking but extremely vulnerable animal from imminent extinction.

1

About the Rhinoceros

THE RHINOCEROS IS among the largest and heaviest land animals alive today. The first rhinoceroses lived over 40 million years ago. The fossil record shows that there have been more than one hundred species of rhinos in the past, varied in size and appearance and adapted to a wide range of habitats and diets. Prehistoric rhinoceroses were found on every continent except South America and Australia. Some ancient rhinos were as small as two feet tall; others were enormous. One species, called *Indricotherium*, was eighteen feet tall and weighed thirty tons. This rhino was hornless and had only four teeth. It is the heaviest land mammal that ever lived, and its fossil has been found in what is now Pakistan. Rhinos became extinct in North America around 5 million years ago, while rhinos in Europe lived until the end of the last Ice Age, around ten thousand years ago. Woolly rhinos were hunted by Stone Age people, who made cave paintings of them, and their preserved carcasses have been found in the Siberian tundra and in European bogs.

Several theories explain the decline of these ancient rhinoceroses. Because they were browsers and ate saplings and leaves, it is possible that their demise is linked to a change in their vegetation zone. If the forests in which they were accustomed to living evolved into grasslands and steppes, they would have suffered. Animals that are too specialized in their feeding preferences die out when their food sources become limited, perhaps by an increase in a competing species or as the result of climatic changes.

Prehistoric wall paintings, found in a cave in southern France, depict rhinos and bison of the glacial era. The two-horned Sumatran rhino is a direct descendant of the woolly rhino of the Stone Age.

Two evolutionary lines

Five distinct species of rhinoceros exist today: the black and white African rhinoceroses, the Sumatran rhinoceros, the Indian rhinoceros, and the Javan rhinoceros. Although they descend from a common ancestor, the five types of rhinoceroses today represent two different evolutionary lines that diverged over 30 million years ago.

During the Oligocene epoch, millions of years before the earliest humans, rhinoceroses split into two distinct groups: the two-horned species and the one-horned species. The evolutionary line that led to the two-horned species included the woolly rhinoceros that lived in Asia and Europe during the Stone Age. The modern two-horned Sumatran rhinoceros is the direct descendant of this Stone Age woolly rhinoceros. Because it has survived nearly unchanged since the Tertiary period (from 65 million years ago until 2 million years ago), the Sumatran rhino of western Indonesia is the most primitive form of rhinoceros alive today. About 10 million years ago, a group of two-horned rhinoceroses migrated to Africa, where they evolved into the black and white rhinoceroses. The second evolutionary line, that of the one-horned species, led to the Indian and Javan rhinoceroses.

Rhinos are ungulates

Today's rhinoceroses are members of an ancient family of animals known as the ungulates, the first mammals to develop hooves. Ungulates are plant eaters and have keen senses of smell and hearing. These passive animals normally react to threat by retreating rather than standing and fighting. Rhinoceroses are among the odd-toed ungulates, known as perissodactyls, a name derived from the Greek word for "odd-fingered." Perissodactyls, from which modern-day horses also descend, originated about 50 million years ago, during the Eocene period. Over the next tens of millions of years, the perissodactyls were gradually outnumbered by the more successful even-toed ungulates, known as artiodactyls, such as deer, antelope, camels, and hippopotamuses. The artiodactyls were faster and smarter than the perissodactyls and therefore held the advantage in competition for food.

Rhinos are also pachyderms, the name for hoofed mammals with thick skin. The word comes from two Greek words: *pachys*, meaning "thick," and *derma*, meaning "skin." Elephants and hippopotamuses are also pachyderms. Although the rhino's thick gray skin appears armorlike, it can be pierced by knives, bullets, and spears, and can also develop sores from biting ticks and flies.

The "nose horn"

All rhinoceroses have characteristics in common, the most distinctive being their facial horns. The rhinoceros takes its name from two Greek words, *rhinos* and *ceros*, meaning "nose horn." A rhinoceros's horn is actually a hard mass of hollow keratin, which is the same material that forms human fingernails. On rhinos, the keratin forms long hairlike fibers that grow into a solid horn fixed over a bony knob on the rhino's skull. African and Sumatran rhinos have two horns; the Indian and Javan rhinos have one.

If the horn is knocked off, it will grow back, particularly on young rhinos. The African rhinos have especially long and pointed horns, which they sharpen on trees and rocks. In two-horned rhinos, the front horn is usually much larger than the rear one. The longest horn on record came from a white rhino and was over six feet long. Rhinos use their horns to fight one another and to ward off predators—

Rhinoceros horns are made up of long, hair-like fibers of keratin, the same material that forms human finger-nails. The keratin fibers grow into a solid horn that will regenerate if knocked off.

though, compared with their prehistoric ancestors who were a food source for ancient animals like saber-toothed tigers, today's rhinos have virtually no carnivorous predators. Sometimes a rhino will use its horns to dig holes in the ground or to hook limbs of vegetation. Male rhinos will also butt horns with one another to determine who is strongest. Males and females sometimes wrestle horns playfully during courtship.

The rhino's role in nature

The rhino's original ecological role as an ungulate was that of a primary consumer. By consuming plant life, rhinoceroses concentrated the plant energy and became a suitable food source for carnivorous predators. Today rhinos no longer have any serious predators, other than humans. Lions and spotted hyenas may prey on young rhinos, but calves are usually protected by their mothers. Rhinos are no longer a significant food source for any other animal, but they do perform vital functions for other animals in their habitat. Some types of rhinoceros help to preserve grasslands for other grazers by consuming saplings and bushes that crop up on the savanna. Because of their size and heavy tread, rhinos are also able to beat paths through the thickest bush, allowing smaller animals access to water holes. Unfortunately, since rhinos are creatures of habit they tend to move along the same paths each day, making it easy for poachers to track and kill them. In addition, rhinos are not stealthy animals, and their tendency to crash through cover makes them easy targets.

A rhino's diet

Rhinos are herbivores; they often feed for fifteen hours a day to consume enough food to keep their bodies running. The rhinoceros digests cellulose, a compound found in the cell walls of plants, by bacterial action in its roomy intestine, or cecum. This arrangement enables it to digest large quantities of fiber. Each rhino needs a large feeding area, so they tend to roam alone rather than in herds. Because they require so much food, rhinos are not "efficient" animals;

they require a lot of space per animal, and even small reductions in habitat affect them adversely. Some rhinos have front teeth that enable them to eat grass, and some rhinos also have a prehensile upper lip designed for grasping leaves. Rhinos have between twenty-four and thirty-four teeth, depending on their species. All rhinos have strong molars, which they use to crush and chew food.

Rhinos drink daily and require a water source within three miles, although the African rhinoceros can go without water for up to three or four days during drought. Since rhinos prefer wet, fertile habitats and need a permanent water source nearby, they suffer in times of drought. Rhinoceroses use water and mud as a means of keeping cool, since they cannot sweat. Rhinos like to wallow in mud and, where possible, make this a daily habit. The mud absorbs the heat from their bodies and provides a protective coating for their skin, helping to keep it supple and to prevent the penetration of ticks and other parasites.

Nearly one-third of a rhino's day is spent sleeping; rhinos can sleep while standing up or lying down. Although rhinoceroses are placid, slow movers in their undisturbed state, they are remarkably agile and flexible for their size. A rhino typically walks at a speed of three miles per hour, and trots at a speed of eighteen miles per hour; however, a rhino can run at a speed of up to thirty miles per hour for short distances, usually while charging or retreating. Like all creatures descended from prey animals, the rhinoceros has highly developed senses of hearing and smell.

Rhino senses

Rhinoceroses have large, rotating ears that can locate the direction of sounds and alert them to potential danger. They issue a variety of grunts, screams, and snorts. Males and females whistle to each other before mating, and mothers and calves communicate with soft, mewing sounds. Researchers believe rhinos may also use low sounds, known as infrasounds, that are inaudible to humans and travel over long distances, allowing the animals to communicate even when they cannot see each other.

A rhino's sense of hearing is important because it has poor eyesight; although it can recognize movement beyond one hundred feet, it can see no detail beyond that distance and is unable to recognize a faraway predator. The rhino's poor eyesight is usually attributed to the fact that it was originally a forest dweller; seeing beyond several feet was rarely necessary.

Despite their thick skin, rhinos suffer from parasites such as ticks and worms, and they often develop what are called "rhino sores" in the soft skin behind their shoulder, which is difficult for them to scratch or rub. The biting fly, a parasite common to rhinos, breeds in rhino dung. When a rhino passes a dung heap, the fly attaches itself to the animal. Tick-eating birds such as egrets, oxpeckers, and mynahs like to perch atop grazing rhinos and feed on parasites in the rhino's skin. The birds also function as an alarm system for the rhinos, flying up and making loud screeching calls at perceived threats.

Rhinos communicate with a variety of snorts, grunts, and whistles. Researchers believe rhinos also have the capability to communicate over long distances with infrasounds, sounds inaudible to humans.

The rhino's powerful sense of smell also enables it to detect threats from a distance, often giving the rhino time to make an escape. Large nostrils and nasal cavities allow rhinos to smell a predator at distances of up to half a mile. Rhinoceroses also use their sense of smell to signal other rhinoceroses. When they rub themselves on trees or brush against bushes, rhinos leave behind flakes of dried skin, which other rhinoceroses can smell. Urine and dung are also powerful scent markers. Alongside trails between feeding and watering areas, rhinos maintain communal dung heaps; each passing rhino, stimulated by the scent of the pile, adds to it. These dung heaps confirm that the trail does lead to a feeding or watering area, and they may also alert rhinos to the population density of an area. Dung and urine also serve as territorial markers. Rhinoceroses urinate in a wide spray, like that from an aerosol can, to increase the area saturated with their scent.

Territoriality

Male rhinos maintain feeding territories that they also use as breeding grounds. A territory's size depends on a rhino population's density but averages about three-quarters of a square mile. Males achieve alpha, or dominant, status through contests of nonlethal horn wrestling. Subsidiary males, who are usually young and not yet capable of replacing a dominant male, are allowed to feed in another male's feeding ground provided they do not get in the way and they are submissive to the alpha male. Unsuccessful adult males must remain subsidiaries, tolerated but not welcomed in an alpha male's territory. Female rhinos may overlap their territories with other females, and females with calves will tolerate each other's presence, but because rhinos require a large grazing area, they tend not to be social animals and usually feed alone. As a result, they do not have the protection of a herd and must fend for themselves.

Breeding

Rhinos mate and give birth throughout the year. When a female is in estrus—the time when she is able to become pregnant—she sprays urine and makes a whistling sound that attracts male rhinos. Cows, or female rhinos, have their first calf around age six and can give birth every two to three years after that. Since the gestation period of a female rhino is very long, an average of sixteen months, they are unable to reproduce quickly. A female breeding at two-to-three-year intervals may bear ten to eleven calves during her life span of forty to fifty years. Compared with other ungulates, this is a very slow rate of reproduction, but since rhinos lack any real threat from animal predators and have developed a system of ritualized rather than actual aggression, their low mortality rates made higher fertility unnecessary. Today, however, with an increase in poaching, their slow rate of reproduction is a serious obstacle to maintaining stable population levels.

Male rhinos, called bulls, mature sexually between ages five and eight, but do not mate successfully until they are around age twelve, when they have grown to their full size and strength and are able to defeat other alpha males as well as overcome female aggression. A male rhino must survive over a decade before it is likely to reproduce, contributing to the slow rate of rhino reproduction. In the wild a calf nurses until it is about two years old, but begins eating plants at only about one week old. For the first two years, females keep their calves hidden and close by until they are strong enough to fend for themselves. Lions, spotted hyenas, crocodiles, and tigers all prey on rhino calves, and if a mother is killed, her calf's chances for survival are slim. Since female rhinos often have longer, thinner horns than males, they too are sought after by poachers. Although rhinos in the wild are capable of living into their fifties, most are killed by poachers before they die of natural causes.

The white rhinoceros

In 1960 Africa was home to 100,000 rhinos; today approximately 7,500 white rhinos and 2,400 black rhinos remain in southern and central Africa. The African white rhino has two subspecies: the seriously endangered northern white, now found only in Congo, and the southern white, which represents the only increasing species of

A white rhinoceros guards her calf as they drink from a watering hole. Females keep their calves nearby until they are old enough to defend themselves.

The Habitat of the White Rhino

rhino, scattered from Kenya to South Africa. White rhinos are the largest of all rhinos. The adult white rhino stands 5 to 6 feet high at the shoulder and weighs 5,000 to 7,900 pounds. The white rhinoceros has a misleading name, for it is the same gray color as the black rhinoceros. Both are two-horned African rhinoceroses; what distinguishes them is the shape of their mouths. The white rhino has a square, wide lip, while the black rhino has a prehensile, grasping upper lip adapted for browsing. The white rhino takes its name from a corruption of the Afrikaans word *weit*, meaning "wide," used to describe its mouth; the black rhino appears to have acquired its name by contrast. The white rhino's flat lip is suited to cropping short grass. White rhinos have two long pointed horns that grow throughout their lives. The length of the front horn can range from 3 to 6½ feet long, but horns over 6 feet are unheard-of today as so few rhinos live long enough to grow lengthy horns.

The black rhinoceros

The black rhino, Africa's other two-horned rhinoceros, has suffered the greatest rate of decline of all the rhinos in recent decades. Since 1970 the world's black rhino population has declined by 96 percent. Today there are only approximately twenty-four hundred black rhinos left in the tropical bushlands and savannas of Africa. The black rhino stands five to six feet tall at the shoulder and weighs up to four thousand pounds. Its front horn averages from eighteen inches to four feet long. Distinguished by its prehensile upper lip, which acts like a small finger, grabbing leaves and twigs, the black rhino browses rather than grazes and occupies a different ecological niche than the white rhino, preferring rugged, hilly terrain and the edges of wooded areas to open grassland. Using its horns, the black rhino pulls branches down to where its lips can reach

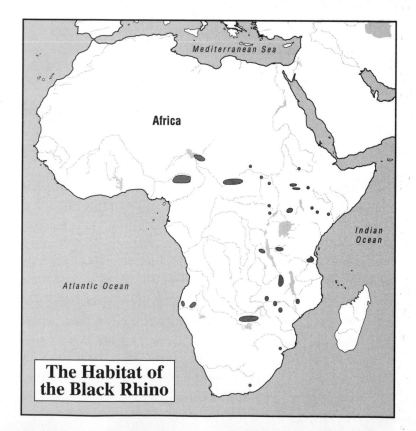

The Habitat of the Black Rhino

them. It also feeds on fallen fruit and on clover that is long enough to be grasped in bundles with its lip. Black rhinos help to improve pastures for grazing animals by feasting on the seedlings of trees.

Considered the most aggressive of all rhinos, black rhinos have been known to charge vehicles and people who get too close to them, and they are capable of reaching speeds of up to thirty miles per hour. The black rhino's reputation for being more fierce can probably be attributed to the animal's habitat. Unlike the white rhino, which feeds on open grassland, the black rhino prefers denser bush and forests. Since movement in the bush is more difficult to sense, the black rhino is more likely to be startled by a human approach—and a startled rhino is an angry rhino.

The black rhino's front horn averages eighteen inches to four feet in length and is used to pull branches down to the rhino's mouth.

The Indian rhinoceros

Although its numbers dropped below two hundred in the twentieth century, today there are more than two thousand Indian rhinoceroses living in the floodplains and swampy grasslands of northern India and southern Nepal. Indian rhinos stand about six feet tall and weigh about four thousand pounds. The Indian rhino has one horn and a unique semiprehensile upper lip that can adapt to a variety of feeding situations in grasslands, wooded areas, and swamplands, where it eats marsh grasses and aquatic plants such as water hyacinth.

The Indian rhinoceros is the largest rhino in Asia. It has knobby skin that is covered with raised round bumps that make it look as though it is wearing armor. At one time the Indian rhino had a wide distribution in Asia, ranging from Pakistan to Myanmar (formerly Burma), where it preferred to roam in river valleys.

Indian rhinos remain in the shade of the forest during the afternoon and head for more open feeding areas as the sun sets. They graze during the evening, and in the early

The Indian rhinoceros population dropped to dangerously low levels in the twentieth century. Although still endangered, over two thousand Indian rhinos, like this seven-week-old calf, roam India and Nepal.

The Indian rhinoceros population dropped to dangerously low levels in the twentieth century. Although still endangered, over two thousand Indian rhinos, like this seven-week-old calf, roam India and Nepal.

morning hours they rest in the feeding area, lying down. Females often choose to rest in tall grass that provides some cover for their young, who are the prey of tigers. Only the young are vulnerable to tiger attacks; healthy adult Indian rhinos have no predators other than humans. As the temperature rises in the late morning, Indian rhinos head for cover; by midday they enter their wallows, where they remain submerged until late afternoon. As many as nine rhinos will wallow together in the same mud holes. Wallows function as public spaces for the Indian rhinoceros, who is not territorial about its watering holes and bathing areas. Indian rhinos maintain private feeding grounds and sleeping areas, but do not patrol them aggressively like African rhinos, nor do they mark their territory with dung and urine. Indian rhinos will fight to defend their area, but feeding grounds are usually large enough that this is unnecessary.

The Javan rhinoceros

Related to the Indian rhinoceros, the Javan rhino stands 4½ to 5½ feet tall and can weigh up to three thousand pounds. Its single horn, found only on males, grows to ap-

proximately ten inches. Seeking extremely remote, dense regions of lowland tropical rain forests, the Javan rhino feeds
at the edges of the forest on bamboo, plants, and fruits.

The Javan rhino is the rarest of all the rhinos; detection
is difficult, but there are now thought to be fewer than one
hundred of this species left in the world. About sixty are
believed to be living in the Ujong Kulon National Park in
Java, and another group of less than forty may still live in
the Cat Loc Nature Reserve in Vietnam. Because there are
none in captivity to be studied, and because they are so difficult to track in the wild, little is known about the biology
of these rhinos. Javan rhinos may be the rarest large mammal in the world.

Javan rhinos once inhabited Sumatra, Malaysia, Thailand, Vietnam, and Burma, but government-sponsored
bounties placed on their heads because of the damage they
caused to farmers' crops, coupled with the market for medicinal products made from rhino horn, decimated their
population.

According to the National Geographic Society, which
led an expedition to Java to study its rhinos in 1985, male

Facts About Rhinos

Species	Average Height at Shoulder	Average Weight	Average Length of Front Horn
White	5–6 ft.	5,000–7,900 lbs.	3–6.5 ft.
Black	5–6 ft.	2,200–4,000 lbs.	1.5–4 ft.
Indian	3.5–6.5 ft.	3,300–4,400 lbs.	8–24 in.
Sumatran	3–5 ft.	700–2,000 lbs.	10–31 in.
Javan	4.5–5.5 ft.	3,000 lbs.	10 in.

Javan rhinos spray bushes with their urine, a habit which marks their territory and identifies it to individuals following the same path. Javan rhinos do not use dung as a signaling device like other species of rhinos. Javan rhinos defecate sporadically, indicating that dung is not a means of communication. With the extinction of the Javan tiger, humans have become the Javan rhino's only predator.

The Sumatran rhinoceros

Almost as rare as the Javan rhino is the Sumatran species, which, despite its greater population, is believed to be the most threatened rhinoceros today because its habitat is rapidly shrinking. The Sumatran rhino is the only Asian species with two horns and the only rhino with hair on its body. It is the smallest of all modern rhinos, standing around 4½ feet tall and weighing from seven hundred to two thousand pounds. The Sumatran rhino's front horn averages from fifteen to twenty inches long; its second horn is often just a bump. A Sumatran rhino is easily distinguished by the reddish brown patches of coarse hair along its back and sides and by the tufts of black hair on the tips of its ears. Scientists believe it is the closest living relative of the woolly rhinoceros. Although it once roamed throughout Southeast Asia, frequently overlapping its range with that of the Javan rhino, today the Sumatran rhino is found only in parts of Indonesia and Malaysia. The Sumatran rhino prefers dense cover and thick vegetation, and it is capable of climbing in steep terrain that antelopes and even humans are unable to navigate. Sumatran rhinos have a prehensile upper lip and are browsers, feeding on leaves, twigs, fruits, and bamboo shoots. The Sumatran has also been observed eating lichen and mushrooms off of trees, as well as grazing on tall grass. Like the Javan, the Sumatran species

The Sumatran rhinoceros is believed to be the closest living relative of the woolly rhino. It is the only rhino with body hair.

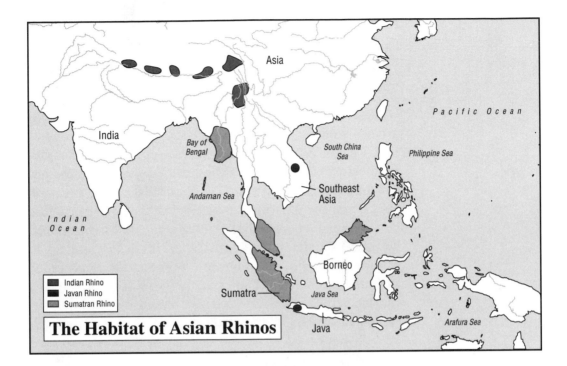

Asia

Pacific Ocean

India

Bay of
Bengal

South China
Sea

Philippine Sea

Andaman Sea

Southeast
Asia

Indian
Ocean

Indian Rhino
Javan Rhino
Sumatran Rhino

Borneo

Sumatra

Java Sea

Arafura Sea

The Habitat of Asian Rhinos

Java

has been seen "walking down" small trees in order to reach the leaves near its top. Sumatran rhinos make tunnels through dense vegetation, and researchers have found rock passages worn smooth by passing rhinos.

The Sumatran rhinoceros has the rhino's characteristic slow rate of reproduction, with a gestation period of about eighteen months. This is one factor in its decline, as is poaching for the medical market. Sumatran rhinos have been hunted for centuries. Sumatran people killed rhinos by laying traps along the steep sides of trails and placing sharply pointed stakes in the ground for the animals to fall on. Pits were also dug along the rhinos' favorite trails and filled with pointed stakes. In Borneo hunters used poisoned blow darts, often tracking a single rhinoceros for weeks at a time. Sumatran rhinos in Borneo and China have been hunted for the medicinal uses of their body parts for hundreds of, possibly even a thousand, years. Until recently, Sumatran rhinos were also the targets of European sport hunting. Today a number of factors contribute to the decline of the species. The continued use of rhinoceros parts in Asian medicine makes the Sumatran rhino a target of poachers, and its habitat continues to be eroded by the expansion of human populations and deforestation.

The last of their kind

Though the estimated eleven thousand remaining rhinos are described as living "in the wild," most survive in national parks or private sanctuaries. As an animal group, rhinoceroses are long past the peak of their evolutionary development. Although they were once the most common land mammals in North America, they became extinct on that continent about 5 million years ago. All living rhinos descend from the Asian and African rhinos that peaked 40 million years ago, when the giant prehistoric rhinos such as *Paraceratherium* and *Indricotherium* browsed the forests and plains of Asia. Swiss zoologist Ernst Lang describes the decline of the modern rhinoceros:

> Compared to this multitude of forms in the Tertiary and glacial rhinoceros, the surviving four genera [some taxonomists lump the related black and white rhinos into one genus] seem rather stunted in spite of their size. They all live in remote habitats, seemingly because they have not been able to compete any longer with the other ungulates, especially the ruminants. Above all, however, human influence has basically changed wide areas of Asia and Africa, thus making them uninhabitable for rhinoceros.

In the long run, the rhino's diminished ability to compete with other hooved mammals has made its extinction inevitable; in the normal course of evolution, we would expect its extinction thousands of years from now. However, human intervention in rhinoceros populations is accelerating the species' extinction. Indeed, exploitation of rhinoceros parts is a worldwide human activity.

2

The Worldwide Use of Rhinoceros Products

COMMERCIAL EXPLOITATION OF the rhinoceros on an unsustainable level is one of the major causes of rhinoceros endangerment today. Rhinoceros horn has had widespread usage throughout history as both a medicine and an ornament: Ancient medical texts attest to its use as an ingredient and ancient ceremonial cups carved from rhino horn have been found in both India and China. However, rhinos did not face extinction until the twentieth century, when demand for rhino products began to outstrip a dwindling supply. The demand for rhinoceros horn and its ever-increasing value in the marketplace continue to fuel the poaching of rhinoceroses. Rhinoceros horn remains a prized commodity in some parts of the world, where it holds symbolic, cultural, and medicinal importance.

The demand for rhinoceros horn daggers

Until recently, one-half of the rhino horn sold in the world ended up in San'a, the capital of the Middle Eastern country of Yemen, where a single black rhino horn can be worth $50,000 or more. In San'a rhino horn is fashioned into handles for ceremonial curved daggers, known as *djambias*. A *djambia* is given to a young Muslim male as an important symbol of manhood. Only the wealthiest members of Yemeni society can afford a rhinoceros horn handle, and owning the genuine article has become a symbol of social status. During the 1970s more than 16,000 pounds of rhino horn were sold in Yemen each year. The dagger trade peaked during the petroleum boom of the 1970s and 1980s when oil-rich Yemenis could afford the horn handles. Between 1969 and 1977, 49,900 pounds of black rhino horn were imported to Yemen from Africa, representing about 8,000 rhinos killed. Between 1970 and 1986, with sustained demand for dagger handles made of rhino horn, the world's black rhino population fell from 65,000 to 4,000. Although an international ban, announced in 1977, forbids the sale of rhino horn, dealers are willing to break the law because the enterprise is so lucrative. Even the shavings from carvers' shops are carefully recovered and sold for medicinal use.

A rhinoceros horn dagger is rarely used as a weapon or tool; its function is primarily decorative and symbolic, of deep cultural significance. Because it is unlikely that Yemeni society could be persuaded to abandon the carrying of *djambias*, efforts to stop use of rhino horn for this purpose have focused on substituting cheaper material, such as cattle horn, and targeting manufacturers and importers. Zoologist Malcolm Penny reports that in 1986 Yemeni government officials and prominent conservationists agreed to the following six-point plan to stop the horn trade:

1. The Yemeni prime minister would personally ask major traders to stop.
2. The Yemeni foreign minister and an official from the United Arab Emirates would address the need to shut down rhino horn trade routes within their countries.
3. Rhino horn shavings could no longer be exported for the medicinal trade.
4. Religious leaders would announce that the willful destruction of a species was against the will of Allah.
5. Dagger makers would not be relicensed if they continued using rhino horn.

6. Water buffalo horn would be encouraged as a substitute for rhino horn dagger handles.

This strategy, coupled with the efforts of conservation organizations like the World Wide Fund for Nature, has worked to dramatically decrease the amount of rhino horn imported to Yemen. By 1993, annual imports of rhino horn to Yemen had dropped from an average of 4,400 pounds in the 1980s to under 220 pounds. Today in Yemen fewer than one dagger handle in a thousand is made from rhino horn.

The medicinal uses of rhinoceros horn

For thousands of years Asian medicine has prescribed rhinoceros horn for a variety of purposes, from reducing fever to stopping convulsions and nosebleeds. A fifteen-hundred-year-old Chinese medical text, *Divine Plowman's Herbal*, records the use of rhino horn for treating fevers and headaches. According to Kai-Yu Wei of Taiwan's Society of Traditional Chinese Medical Doctors, rhino horn is also prescribed to "clear away heat and remove toxic materials, and to cool the blood and stop bleeding." Today, powdered rhino horn is an important ingredient in traditional

At a pharmacy in Hong Kong, powder from this rhinoceros horn may be prescribed for fever, convulsions, or headaches.

Asian medicines prescribed to treat fevers, headaches, colds, and other disorders. Medicines containing rhino horn are manufactured in the form of powders, pills, and tonics, and have a worldwide distribution, although the main consumers are China, Korea, Taiwan, Singapore, Malaysia, and Hong Kong, as well as Asian communities in the United States and Europe. A recent survey in Taiwan revealed that 77 percent of traditional pharmacies continued to stock rhino horn, and 41 percent of licensed doctors continued to prescribe rhino horn to their patients.

This widespread perceived benefit, however, appears to have no basis in fact. According to the World Wide Fund for Nature, scientists from the Swiss pharmaceutical firm Hoffmann–La Roche concluded after testing that rhino horn had no medicinal effect on humans. Some Chinese scientists have found that rhino horn did have a cooling effect on fever, but only when administered in enormous doses to laboratory rats.

Other rhinoceros remedies

There has been a long-standing misconception in the West that rhino horn is prized as an aphrodisiac in Asia. Although rhino horn itself is not used for this purpose, rhino and tiger penises have long been touted as aphrodisiacs and continue to be sold for this purpose in Laos, Thailand, Taiwan, China, and India. Consumers believe they will gain the sexual prowess of these animals by ingesting their genitals. An expensive specialty, tiger penis soup is still served in some Taiwanese restaurants, despite the fact that the tiger is also an endangered species.

In his book *Rhino Exploitation*, Esmond Bradley Martin details some of the disorders for which rhinoceros parts are prescribed throughout Asia, including fever, headache, and typhus. To treat these ailments, rhino horn is shaved and then boiled in water, which is strained and given to the patient to drink. Sometimes hoof shavings, which are less costly, are substituted for horn shavings, or water buffalo horn is substituted for rhino horn. Rhinoceros hide is also considered useful among the Chinese for curing skin diseases; the hide is likewise boiled and the patient drinks the water. Water buffalo hide is sold as an acceptable but less desirable substitute to those who cannot afford rhino hide. Since dealers sometimes swindle unsuspecting consumers by substituting buffalo hide for the real thing, some customers will pay more to watch as the hide is cut from the rhino, safeguarding against fraud.

Traditional Indian medicine also assigns many uses to rhino horn, including treating hemorrhoids, arthritis, and lumbago. Rhinoceros blood, dung, and urine are also used to treat skin disorders and muscular aches. Rhino blood has been used as a tonic in India. To cure a stiff neck, some people mix rhinoceros dung with eucalyptus oil and rub it over the affected area. Rhino urine is used externally as an aphrodisiac and taken internally to cure coughs and sore throats in India and Nepal. Rhino dung and urine are actually sold by some Indian zoos as a means of generating revenue for rhino conservation.

In 1992, more than eleven hundred pounds of rhino horn were used as a fever remedy. Today the World Wildlife Fund (WWF) estimates that 60 percent of traditional pharmacies in East Asia stock rhino horn. Usually sold in powdered form, rhino horn is one of the most expensive substances in the world, with a street value higher than gold. Since a single African rhino carries from four to eleven pounds of horn, it is a prize target of hunters. Middlemen who organize the illegal trade reap most of the profits, however. Poachers, who risk their lives by breaking the law, receive only a fraction of the income that a rhinoceros horn will eventually generate.

The international trade in endangered species

A grisly business, the trade in illegal animal parts ranges from the sale of tiger penises and skulls in China to rhinoceros dung, urine, hide, and horn, made possible by organized underground networks of poachers, dealers, salespeople, and consumers. A former rhino dealer from Taiwan told the Endangered Species Project that he and his business associates bought ten tons of rhino horn on the streets

Chinese medicine is known for using a variety of objects, including rhinoceros horn, to cure ailments. This shop sells rhino horns, deer antlers, rare shellfish, and other objects for medicinal use.

of Taiwan in 1988, cornering the domestic market and driving the price of horn from $700 per pound up to $2,700 per pound within a few months.

The impending extinction of the rhinoceros apparently does not alarm traders, who are hoarding horn in the hopes of selling it for exorbitant prices when their supply becomes the last available. There may be as many as thirty-six thousand pounds of illegal rhino horn stockpiled already in China and Taiwan. As the Environmental Investigation Agency reported in 1993: "Now, with a street value higher than gold for some varieties, dealers are stockpiling horn and speculating on the extinction of the species."

Trade Record Analysis of Flora and Fauna (TRAFFIC), which is affiliated with the World Wildlife Fund, has researched these trade networks. TRAFFIC agents pose as wealthy buyers and collectors, gathering information on the availability and prices of illegal animal parts. A 1990 study commissioned by TRAFFIC revealed that there were at least ten tons of rhinoceros horn on pharmacy shelves in Taiwan.

"An enormous international trade in endangered species flows into Southeast Asia," says Sam LaBudde, director of the Endangered Species Project.

> There are other major trade routes for endangered wildlife, such as parrots and other birds coming up out of Africa and Latin America into European and American pet stores, but the vast majority of the trade flows into and out of South Korea, China, Singapore, Vietnam, Hong Kong, and above all, Taiwan.

The use of rhinoceros parts in Asian medicine is the major impetus behind poaching. However, those who seek to punish Asian pharmacists for selling illegal goods to consumers have been accused of ignoring cultural sensitivities and launching a campaign hostile to Asian medicine. Sam LaBudde believes that rhino horn does, in enormous doses, have some success in reducing fever, but he also maintains that the treatment is far less effective and far more expensive than ordinary aspirin. More importantly, LaBudde maintains, "these species do not belong to the Taiwanese. They do not belong to anyone."

Rhinoceros parts are also being sold illegally in the United States. According to Kenyan rhino activist Michael Werikhe, who has conducted walking campaigns throughout his native Kenya to educate people about the plight of the rhinoceros, "A lot of it comes into the Chinatowns. You can buy rhino-horn pills in just about any Chinatown in the U.S. You don't have to go to Asia to get it." A 1995 survey of nine Los Angeles stores specializing in Asian items found that six of them carried rhino-based products.

Alternatives to rhino horn

The persistence of the rhino horn trade has shown that the demand for products and medicines made from rhino horn is not simply a passing fad. Recognizing that humans have used rhino horn for centuries and that entrenched beliefs and attitudes are not changed overnight, organizations like the WWF and TRAFFIC are sponsoring research into alternative medicines that can replace rhino horn, but which are similar to or based on traditional Chinese medical practices. In this way, the needs of people and rhinos can be balanced. Water buffalo horn and hide, for example, have been touted as possible substitutes for rhino products.

Raising public awareness

Through educational programs, conservationists hope to raise public awareness about the effect that the demand for rhino horn has on the rhino population. "Above all," says the WWF, "the link between the illegal trade in rhino horn medicine and the disastrous effect it is having on the world's endangered rhinos must be made clear through culturally sensitive publicity campaigns, particularly in consuming countries."

Alarmed by what appeared to be an increasing interest in rhino products in the United States, the U.S. Fish and Wildlife Service began an educational campaign targeted at Asian immigrants. Radio and print advertisements in

This endangered wildlife exhibit of skins travels to museums displaying a variety of items confiscated by the U.S. Fish and Wildlife Service as illegal trade.

Asian languages, together with workshops, posters, and brochures, warned consumers of the potential for rhinoceros extinction. Los Angeles was targeted by the federal program because of its large Asian immigrant population. In addition to funding educational programs, the Fish and Wildlife Service also supports international rhino conservation efforts through funding and technical assistance, including research and resource management.

"Almost all the conservation efforts for bigger species—tigers, rhinos, elephants, pandas, bears—have been focused on protectionist efforts in the range states," maintains the director of the Endangered Species Project. "Hardly anyone has said boo to the consuming nations, where the actual problem resides. We treat symptoms instead of causes." While loss of habitat remains a significant reason for rhinoceros decline, overexploitation caused by the demand for rhinoceros products continues to be the major cause of their endangerment. Through educational programs that teach people the effect their actions have on the populations of endangered species, conservationists hope to overcome powerful deep-seated beliefs, customs, and attitudes.

Monitoring the trade

Organizations such as TRAFFIC, the Environmental Investigation Agency, and the Endangered Species Project are working to stop the trade in endangered wildlife products. By gathering information about the buying and selling of rhino horn, they hope to monitor the trade and persuade the governments of countries involved, as well as ordinary people, that the trade in rhino horn should be stopped. Singapore, Yemen, and Taiwan have all banned the trade in rhino horn, but poaching and smuggling continue. "The problem is not the laws," says Sam LaBudde. "There are great laws for wildlife conservation in Taiwan. The trouble is that nobody enforces them, or even knows they exist, most of the time." Simply signing a treaty or enacting a law to ban the rhino trade seems to have had little effect. Hong Kong, for example, banned the trade in rhino horn in 1989, but it continues to be identified as a major exporter of medicines made from rhinoceros parts. Several of the 130 countries that have signed the 1977 CITES treaty banning the trade in endangered animal parts—including Taiwan, China, South Korea, and Yemen—continue to maintain a trade in rhinoceros products.

The Endangered Species Project sends operatives with tiny video recorders into shops selling endangered animal products. Their film of rhino horn powder, rhino hide, panda skins, tiger skulls, and sometimes even live endangered specimens for sale proves to the rest of the world that an illegal business is being conducted, despite laws or treaties indicating otherwise. Information learned about illegal trade networks within consuming nations can also prove useful to policy makers, who can use this knowledge to make their enforcement of CITES more effective.

Visiting a pharmacy or shop where endangered animal products are sold can be a startling experience for the uninitiated. "You've got powdered things in jars," says Sam LaBudde, who has traveled in East Asia looking for evidence of trade in endangered wildlife. "You've got bins with bones, and loose bones lying around. You've got horn, both powdered and in whole form on the shelves. It's sort of like a produce section for wildlife. It smells like a museum. It smells like death."

To force people to stop participating in the rhino horn trade, the U.S. government has imposed economic sanctions on countries where the trade in illegal animal parts flourishes.

Imposing economic sanctions

To halt the poaching of rhinoceroses, as well as that of Asian tigers, the Merchant Marine and Fisheries Commission of the House of Representatives approved a 1994 bill that provided $10 million annually to promote conservation programs in the animals' home countries. Countries deemed lax in stemming the illegal trade in endangered wildlife parts may become the target of U.S. economic sanctions. In August 1994, President Bill Clinton signed

into law the first U.S. sanctions against another country—Taiwan, seat of the Nationalist Republic of China—for its trade in endangered species. Information gathered by undercover operatives in Taiwan was instrumental to the U.S. government's landmark decision to impose economic sanctions under the terms of the Pelly Amendment, a protection act that provides the United States with a two-stage process in which to express disapproval toward an offending nation. The first stage is to identify and blacklist a country as one where the rhino horn trade operates, and the second stage, after an official warning, is to enact economic sanctions. All Taiwanese fish and wildlife exports—primarily snakeskin and coral—were prohibited from U.S. importation. Mainly a slap on the wrist, the sanctions cost Taiwan only about $23 million in annual trade—one-tenth of 1 percent of Taiwan's total annual exports to the United States—but they were symbolically important as the first imposition of economic sanctions beyond censure. And in fact, after the sanctions were levied, the Taiwanese government began a crackdown on the illegal trade. Inspectors were ordered to confirm that pharmacies are in compliance with the ban on the sale of rhino horn and tiger bone. Shops that pass government inspection display stickers in their windows featuring pictures of a rhino and a tiger with the exclamation, "We don't trade tiger products and rhinoceros horn here." In June 1995, after Taiwan showed proof that it was trying to crack down on dealers and stop the use and trade of rhino products, the sanctions were lifted. However, organizations such as TRAFFIC, the Endangered Species Project, and the WWF remain skeptical about the level of law enforcement in Taiwan.

The difficulty of controlling rhino horn trade

The use of rhinoceros horn is a major issue in the arena of international trade. Countries wishing to trade with the United States now have to prove that they are not just hiding behind the law, but that they are taking steps to control the horn trade within their borders. Organizations like the Environmental Investigation Agency, the Endangered Species Project, and TRAFFIC work to gather information that can be used to determine whether consuming nations are really working to control the horn trade.

For example, South Korea's move to join CITES in 1993 was heralded as a triumph by the international community, but despite a supposed crackdown on the trade in rhino parts, TRAFFIC continues to uncover South Korean shops selling rhino horn products. The South Korean trade is estimated to be 650 pounds a year, or 100 rhinos. Currently several countries are threatening to impose trade sanctions against Yemen, South Korea, and China for violating the CITES agreement.

Not all conservationists agree that a trade ban on rhino horn is helping to reduce poaching. Some believe that the difficulty of obtaining rhino horn only serves to drive the prices up and create a greater incentive for dealers to continue to be involved in the trade. The ever increasing price of rhino horn has provided an incentive for the internationally organized poaching rings that have devastated African rhino populations.

3

Poachers and Wardens at War

A POACHER IS a hunter who kills game on land that does not belong to him, in defiance of the law. In the first half of the twentieth century, when the colonial governments in Africa first imposed restrictions on the hunting of certain species, it was to protect the white man's sport of trophy hunting. Naturalist Malcolm Penny notes that the effect of these laws was that "rural tribesmen could not legally hunt any more on land which had been their larder for generations. The hunters whose activities were essential for the survival of their villages were branded 'poachers' and regarded by the authorities as criminals." Indigenous people, however, often regarded the poachers and their acts of defiance as heroic, especially when they killed animals that had been destroying village crops. Poachers thus earned the gratitude and collaboration of many people. Today poachers are still welcomed in many areas because they pay villagers well for performing small services, such as helping to track animals.

A single rhinoceros horn is worth more than a year's wages to a poacher, a tremendous incentive for someone who does not have many other opportunities to earn money. The decline of economies in countries like Zambia has had an enormous impact on the level of poaching in neighboring areas. Zambians who were earning less than the equivalent of $1.50 a day could earn as much as $500 for each horn they brought to the middlemen who run the poaching operations. The possibility of earning a year's worth of money during just one hunting expedition has led many people to risk their lives attempting to poach rhinos. When Zambian poachers depleted their own country's rhino population, they began to poach in the neighboring countries of Zimbabwe and Namibia, whose governments responded by enacting such drastic measures as dehorning rhinos and establishing shoot-on-sight policies regarding poachers. Poaching and antipoaching forces continue to wage a guerrilla war in rhinoceros territory. Each side is heavily armed and prepared to shoot the other. In many cases, poachers, who have more money backing them up, are more heavily armed and more numerous than park guards and scouts. Both sides are risking their lives in the war for the rhino, but a guard's salary of $80 a month is little incentive to join the antipoaching force.

Poachers usually kill rhinos by shooting them, although electrocution is practiced in some areas where poachers are able to lay wires connected to power lines. After killing the rhino, poachers remove the animal's horns and hooves with a saw and may take rhino hide or marketable organs as well, but the rest of the carcass is left behind to rot. To avoid detection by park guards who will shoot them on sight, poachers work as quickly as possible.

To a poacher in Zambia, a rhinoceros horn is worth a tremendous amount of money—more than a year's salary. In contrast, an antipoaching guard earns only $80 a month.

No area where rhinos live is immune to poaching activity. Poachers have even penetrated remote regions of tropical forest in search of rhinos. In Sumatra, researchers trying to estimate the Sumatran rhino population of Danum Valley found that no matter how far they traveled into the forest, they found evidence of hunters. Old campsites and machete cuts marking trails into the forest showed old activity, while current campsites with extended caches of food and supplies, strategically located near rhino trails, indicated recent activity.

As long as the demand for rhinoceros parts exists, ambitious individuals will try to profit from their sale. In the northeast Indian state of Assam, the rhinoceros has become a casualty of a civil war—killed to finance a rebel independence movement.

Rebel movements threaten rhinos

In Assam, which is home to two-thirds of the world's two thousand Indian rhinos, Bodo rebels are poaching Indian rhinos and funneling profits from the sale of rhino horns into their war for independence from India. With one Indian rhino horn selling for tens of thousands of dollars, the rebels are able to purchase enough automatic weapons and explosives for their entire army. Rhino hunting was banned in India in 1954, but today's poachers continue to sell horns to Bhutanese smugglers, who bring the horns into Asian countries. In 1993 a Bhutanese woman was arrested by Hong Kong customs officials when she tried to smuggle twenty-two Indian rhino horns into the country. In 1987, before Bodo rebels occupied Manas, on the border between Bhutan and India, there were as many as one hundred rhinos in the Manas wildlife sanctuary. The International Rhino Foundation believes there are now fewer than four rhinos left in Manas. Bodo poachers shoot or electrocute the rhinos, often laying wires connected to power lines along their favorite paths. Achintia Barua, owner of tourist lodgings in Assam's Kaziranga Sanctuary for rhinos, was quoted in the *Earth Island Journal:*

[The poachers'] organization and the caliber of their guns suggest wealthy backers. The guns the sanctuary's forest officers have confiscated are mostly from China. I think Chinese businessmen pay people from Nagaland—who are famous for their hunting skills—to poach rhino horns in Kaziranga. Men from around the sanctuary, who know the terrain and habits of the rhinos, must also be involved.

The civil war in Zaire, which resulted in the creation of the Democratic Republic of Congo, also placed the tiny population of northern white rhinoceroses—the smallest subspecies of rhinos—at risk. During the conflict, the World Wildlife Fund appealed to the Zairean government and to the rebels to keep their conflict out of the national parks and reserves, particularly the Garamba National Park in the northwest region of Zaire/Congo, which is home to the world's only population of northern white rhinos, a genetically distinct subspecies of the African white rhino. However, poaching rhinos provided rebels with a way to fund their armies. The ongoing civil war in neighboring Sudan has also taken its toll on the region's wildlife, as more than eighty thousand Sudanese refugees have settled in camps surrounding Garamba National Park. Southern Sudanese rebels have poached rhinos, elephants, and buffalo from Garamba and other parks to raise money for their independence movement from Islamic northern Sudan. As of 1996 there were fewer than twenty-nine northern white rhinos in Garamba National Park. And in the spring of 1996, two of these rare northern white rhinos were poached. The two rhinos, a male and a pregnant female, were found dead with their horns sawed off. They were the first northern whites to be poached in twelve years, and their deaths postponed efforts to establish a second wild herd of the animals. According to Claude Martin, general director of the World Wide Fund for Nature,

> With less than 30 individuals left, each animal poached is a severe blow to the chances of survival of this species. The government of Zaire has to do everything in its power to stop the poaching that is putting this species at the edge of extinction.

A level of political stability is essential to gauge the effectiveness of wildlife conservation projects; conservation programs cannot operate in a vacuum, but need to take into account local conditions and problems and what effect they have on wildlife and their habitat. Poverty and civil unrest in the range countries are powerful forces driving poaching. Corruption and mismanagement also undermine the best conservation efforts. Unless they are enforced, laws concerning the protection of rhinos can have no effect.

Shoot-on-sight policies

Zimbabwe, formerly home to more than 3,000 black rhinos—Africa's largest population of that species—was nearly devastated by poaching in the early 1980s; today fewer than 315 black rhinos remain. In 1984 the government of Zimbabwe began to fight back against poachers through a program called Operation Stronghold, which authorized government patrols to shoot poachers on sight. The program was a military-style antiguerrilla campaign against poaching, and it resulted in numerous arrests, the confiscation of weapons and horns, and the deaths of 178 poachers. But poachers outnumbered Zimbabwe's armed guards, and the government could not afford to equip or hire reinforcements. Operation Stronghold slowed but could not stop poachers, many of whom were unemployed men willing to risk death in exchange for the great profits of the horn trade. Zimbabwe abandoned the program in the late 1980s; in the 1990s, it has focused on relocating rhinos to safer habitats as a means of protecting them. Despite frequent patrols, the presence of armed guards, and strict penalties and jail sentences, poaching remains a serious problem in Zimbabwe, as well as in the national parks of Nepal, India, and South Africa. In desperation, some countries have turned to controversial dehorning programs to devalue rhinos and protect them from poaching.

Dehorning

The African black rhino population, which once ranged from Sudan to South Africa, has been hit hardest by poachers. In the early 1970s, as many as sixty-five thousand

black rhinos roamed the continent, but today there are only about twenty-five hundred left, and decline continues. In 1991, desperate to undermine poachers and bolster the black rhino's dwindling numbers, the parks and game departments of the governments of Namibia and Zimbabwe tried a radical approach: removing the horns from black rhinoceroses to so devalue them that they are not worth poaching. The dehorning initiative was conducted in conjunction with an improvement in law enforcement and a clustering of rhinos in protected zones. Experienced veterinarians conducted the dehorning, which involved darting rhinos with tranquilizers and then removing 70 to 80 percent of their front and rear horns with a hand- or chainsaw. The stubs of the horns were then coated with antiseptic and filed smooth. The effect dehorning might have on rhino behavior, however, was unknown; the approach was also highly experimental since biologists were uncertain what advantages the horned animals held over the hornless ones.

Researchers found that a rhino's front horn grows back at a rate of nearly 2½ inches per year, while the rear horn grows 1 inch per year, providing a total of 3½ inches

Poachers have reduced the black rhino population from more than 3,000 to fewer than 315. Here, antipoaching rangers in Zambia display seized poaching rifles, rhino horns, and ivory.

of horn annually—still enough to attract poachers. To make horn removal an effective deterrent, it was necessary to dehorn rhinos each year, at a cost of about $1,400 per rhino. In some cases, dehorning was also found to affect the rhinos' ability to defend their young from predators such as spotted hyenas and lions. Results in Zimbabwe were mixed, but in Namibia, calves born to dehorned mothers tended to die before the age of one, while 100 percent of horned mothers were successful in rearing calves beyond infancy.

"If dehorning continues as a conservation strategy, whether as a short- or long-term measure," note researchers Joel Berger and Carol Cunningham, who studied the dehorned population in Namibia, "it may mean that dehorning should be restricted to areas that lack dangerous predators or it may mean hyenas will have to be killed."

More protective measures

Among the other problems associated with the practice, dehorning does not always deter poachers, who have killed rhinos for the still-valuable stubs of their horns. Poachers have even been known to shoot hornless rhinos simply to avoid wasting time tracking a hornless animal in the future. And in some terrain poachers may not notice a rhino has been dehorned. According to Kenyan wildlife activist Michael Werikhe, "Dehorning is not a solution in the savanna, where there is a lot of vegetation cover. Where there's heavy vegetation, many poachers sneak up on the rhinos and shoot them from behind, before looking to see if they have horns." Since 1983 at least ninety-four dehorned rhinos have been killed by poachers. Sam LaBudde, director of the Endangered Species Project, believes the doggedness with which rhinos are killed is a deliberate attempt by those in the trade to extinguish the African species so the price of Asian rhino horn will skyrocket. Many wildlife officials in Africa are now lobbying for the right to sell their stockpiles of rhino horn, particularly from the large southern white rhino population, believing that a glut in the market will decrease the need for poaching.

Whether laws banning the horn trade can truly help to protect rhinos has become a subject of much debate.

To further protect their rhino populations, national parks and wildlife commissions in Kenya, Zimbabwe, Namibia, and elsewhere have relocated rhinos, moving them from areas where protecting them from poachers was difficult to areas where they can be effectively guarded. This process is called translocation, and the places where rhinos are relocated are called "intensive protection zones," or IPZs. Intensive protection zones may be on government or private land. Increasingly, African parks and game commissions have collaborated with citizens who have an interest in conservation and the resources to fund rhino protection. Governments have placed their rhinos in private sanctuaries, which have proven to be among the safest places for wildlife. Wildlife agencies have also discovered that the cooperation of local people, those who live adjacent to rhino populations, is essential for their conservation strategy to be successful.

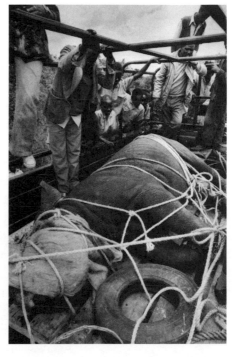

A rhinoceros sleeps with its head wrapped in cloth as it is relocated to an intensive protection zone in Kenya. The translocation process is part of a government program to protect rhinos from poachers.

Legalizing the rhino horn trade

In 1977 signers of the CITES treaty banned the sale of rhinoceros products, but the ban, endorsed by 130 countries—including some of the Asian consumer nations—has not stopped poaching nor has it lessened the value of rhino horn. Many wildlife officials in Africa oppose the trade ban on rhino horn, arguing that a plentiful supply of legitimately acquired horn would decrease demand and lead to a reduction in poaching. They also question whether international pressure has had any effect in slowing the horn trade, or if it has merely forced the market underground, making the rhino trade even more difficult to monitor. Economists have argued in favor of legalization, believing a trade ban hurts rhino conservation by causing the price of horn to escalate and by reducing the ability of wildlife personnel to pay for conservation expenses. Proponents of legalization propose lifting the CITES ban so that horns amassed through dehorning programs can be sold to raise funds for rhino conservation. Others advocate private ownership of rhinos so they can be ranched to supply horn and other products to the market, while preventing their extinction.

Legalization controversy

Opponents of legalization question whether legalizing the horn trade will drive prices down enough to curb poaching. And they are concerned that legalization may lead to an increased demand for rhino products. Although an international ban on ivory has helped control elephant poaching, many conservationists do not believe that a ban on the rhino horn trade can be effective. "Unfortunately there are some significant differences between ivory and rhino horn," says Kenyan wildlife activist Michael Werikhe.

> It's much easier to control the ivory trade, because it's an ornament. Tourists will stay away from ivory ornaments because they know they cannot bring them back into the U.S. Also, it becomes a bit distasteful, to buy something that is looked upon with contempt by society. But the rhino horn is easily ground into powder, it's easy to hide, and, because it's in such demand, its value is higher than ivory's. Also, the usage is on a wider scale. Many cultures consider it a traditional medicine. That's what makes it so difficult to stop.

African wildlife officials who have witnessed failed guerrilla warfare, dehorning, and translocation programs are beginning to lobby for the legalization of trade in rhinoceros parts, believing it may be the only way to curb poaching. If rhino horn were readily available, these officials believe, demand for the product would slow down. "Since the CITES ban on selling rhino horn has failed to stop the traders, the survival of rhino lies in legalizing trade in rhino horn," says Dick Pittman, chairperson of the Zambezi Society, an environmental group in Zimbabwe. Legalization advocates want to use money raised through the sale of rhino horns to pay for the protection of the rhinos and to fund projects in rural communities, thereby helping to place a value on local wildlife conservation. Proponents also support the farming of rhinos for their horns. Rhinos bred on game ranches could generate revenue from tourists, and the combined profits from tourism and the sale of rhino horns could be used to fund conservation programs as well as community development. Stockpiles of confiscated rhino horn, currently held by national parks commissions, could also be sold.

Nan Schaffer, founder of SOS Rhino, an organization dedicated to heightening awareness of rhinoceros endangerment, believes that a legal trade in rhino products might be able to prevent poaching:

> Few animals in the world have an economic incentive to match the 'good as gold' natural resource as the rhino. This should have been the easiest mammal in the world to save. It's one of the top 5 animals that tourists want to see when they go to Africa. The black market is entrenched, well-financed, well-supported, and has been obviously unaffected by legalities. A well-organized and financed legal source can act as enforcement agents, undercut the competition from the black market and drive down the price. . . . Now, the black market gets all the money. A legal trade could monitor the traffic, protect their own 'rhino investment,' and a rhino would not have to be killed.

Many African wildlife officials are lobbying for the right to sell their stockpiles of southern white rhinoceros horn, like these pictured here. Opponents, however, fear that the legalization of the rhino horn trade will only increase the demand and will not curb poaching, as the lobbyists suggest.

However, Schaffer notes, "Others believe that a legal trade will only help the black market survive by creating an accessible trade route. The pros and cons are an ongoing debate in the international community." Any decision to legalize the horn trade would likely come from the members of CITES, who convene annually.

In 1994 South Africa successfully lobbied CITES for permission to allow trophy hunting among its southern white rhino population—the only rhino population to increase significantly in recent years. In contrast to the declining number of black rhinos, southern white rhino

Big-game hunters who really care about the future.

populations in Africa have increased dramatically in this century. Numbered at only twenty in 1895, today there are more than seventy-eight hundred southern white rhinos, most of them living in South Africa. Though the International Union for the Conservation of Nature (IUCN) currently classifies southern white rhinos as being at lower risk than other rhinos, the union cautions that southern whites remain "conservation dependent."

Approximately forty to forty-five southern white rhinos are hunted by permit each year in South Africa, bringing in hundreds of thousands of dollars for rhino conservation. Most of the hunters come from the United States and Europe and are willing to pay steep fees for the chance at a rhinoceros trophy. In 1997 CITES denied South Africa's request to establish a legal trade in southern white rhino horn, which would have allowed the Natal Parks Board there to sell its cache to raise funds for conservation. That same year CITES granted Zimbabwe, Namibia, and Botswana permission to sell their stockpiled ivory to Japan, a country that has long expressed an interest in rhino horn. The ivory trade ban will be lifted for these countries in 1999, but it could be reinstated if they do not continue to meet the CITES requirements.

Involving local populations

Conservationists have tried to provide incentives for people in Africa and Asia who live side by side with rhinoceroses—and in some cases compete with rhinos for land—to help save their habitat. Indigenous people must earn a living so they can feed their own families before they can be concerned about an animal. To ensure the rhino's future, local peoples must come to view live rhinos as more valuable than dead ones. Recognizing this, conservationists such as Willie Nduku of the Department of Parks and Wildlife Management in Zimbabwe have begun to provide reasons for local people to support the rhino population. In Zimbabwe the funneling of tourism revenues into local projects such as the construction of schools and wells gives local people a stake in the preservation of

Zimbabwean conservationists who are trying to earn the support of the indigenous people point out that rhinos are among the top five animals that tourists in Africa wish to see. Tourism revenues continue to increase and are used to build schools and wells for the local people, thereby placing a greater worth on living rhinos and deterring the natives from poaching.

the rhino. As Philip Chigumeta, a council member of the Shangaan tribe, told one reporter, "To us, rhino are worth a lot more alive than dead." However, joint use of land can lead to conflicts when the needs of multiple users are not respected.

Friends of Conservation (FOC) has been helping to fund conservation education programs among the Masai people in Kenya, who live near the boundaries of game reserves. FOC tries to balance the needs of local people with those of the wildlife that share their habitat. By operating public awareness programs in primary and secondary schools, FOC hopes to encourage the Masai to conserve natural resources and make sustainable decisions about the future of their land and wildlife.

But abstract public awareness programs sometimes give way to pragmatic bargaining at the local level. The Masai graze their cattle on rhino territory and are sometimes well paid by poachers for information about rhinos or help in tracking them. Some conservancies have begun to make counteroffers as incentives to leave the rhinos alone. One African conservancy's policy is to pay locals ten times what a poacher has offered, in exchange for turning in the poacher.

Habitat loss threatens rhinos

By itself, curbing poaching is not sufficient action to save the rhinoceros. Rhinos also face the pressures of habitat loss. Expanding human populations in Asia and Africa continue to threaten rhino populations as additional lands are cleared for residential, agricultural, and industrial use. Habitat loss is another crucial threat to overcome if rhinos are to be saved from extinction.

4

The Environmental Threat to the Rhinoceros

RHINOS ARE LARGE animals that eat 1 to 2 percent of their body weight daily; as a result, they require a habitat able to support the immense needs of a rhino population. This type of environment is becoming increasingly difficult for rhinos to find in their range states as human populations continue to encroach into their territory. Across Asia and Africa, vast tracts of rhinoceros habitat have been cleared and developed by human beings for agricultural, commercial, and residential use.

Seventy-seven percent of the world's population was concentrated in the developing world in 1990, but by the year 2025, the population of developing countries is expected to make up over 84 percent of the world's population. This population boom dates to the beginning of the twentieth century, when mortality rates in the developing world dropped off due to improvements in health care, medicine, and sanitation. Since birthrates remained high while death rates fell, the result was increased population growth. Overpopulation leads to overexploitation of resources and myriad social and environmental problems that threaten human populations, their environment, and wild creatures of all kinds. Land has multiple uses and many living things compete for the ability to use it, but human beings have been the most successful in the competition for land, often to the disadvantage of animal populations.

In the late nineteenth and early twentieth centuries, trophy hunters in Africa killed many rhinoceroses, but the decline of rhinos at that time was due largely to habitat loss as lands were cleared and through hunting, which prepared land for settlement. Following the 1940s, so much land in Africa was converted for agricultural use that the number of rhinos declined precipitously. Notorious game hunter John A. Hunter alone killed over sixteen hundred rhinos by order of the Kenyan government.

In Asia, as former grazing grounds of the Indian rhino were turned into rice paddies to feed an expanding human population, rhinos were killed by farmers who consider the animals nuisances because they eat crops and damage the rice fields. Hunting rhinos for the medicinal properties associated with their horn and other body parts also caused the Indian rhino population to dwindle, as did European trophy hunting during India's colonial period. Today there

Because rhinos eat 1 to 2 percent of their body weight per day, they require an immense habitat capable of supporting their needs. Human development of the rhinoceroses' habitat for economic, residential, and agricultural reasons is becoming a serious threat to the rhinos.

ROTHCO
ORIGINAL

"FRANKLY, PROFESSOR, I THINK WE'RE THE ONLY
ENDANGERED SPECIES AROUND HERE!"

are eight reserves in northern India and Nepal that continue to support the Indian rhino population, which has made a comeback despite the persistence of poaching. In Java, however, the expansion of the lumber industry has destroyed much of the forest inhabited by the Javan rhino.

If rhinos are to be saved, conservationists must preserve their habitat and the ecosystem in which they live. Thus, saving the Sumatran rhino, for example, will also mean saving portions of the Indonesian rain forest, where tens of thousands of other species make their home. To help accomplish this goal, developed nations such as the United States and Britain have provided technical assistance for wildlife conservation in developing countries. Establishing and maintaining protected areas is an essential component of conservation.

Habitat protection

One of the first steps in establishing a protection and management plan for rhinos is to conduct a population and distribution survey. This helps wildlife managers determine where rhinos are located and identify their population density. Rhinos may then be translocated to national parks or private sanctuaries where they can roam safely.

Fragmented rhino populations may also be grouped and moved to areas where they can interact and reproduce, helping to ensure greater genetic diversity. Wildlife managers must ensure that the rhino's habitat provides sufficient vegetation, minerals, water, and space for the number of animals it carries. The habitat must also protect against encroachment by humans—a difficult measure to uphold in the range states where expanding human populations are faced with resource shortages that force them into rhino territory.

Political and agricultural factors

Catastrophes such as droughts, floods, wars, and ensuing problems of refugee migrations can affect the livelihood of human populations and disrupt efforts to conserve rhino habitat. Recent political upheavals in countries like Rwanda, Zaire, and Sudan have ravaged both human and wildlife populations and their habitat. Driven from their homes, refugees often establish makeshift camps in wildlife reserves because of the abundance of uninhabited land. By living in such close proximity to wildlife, they compete for the same scant resources the habitat offers. Refugees seeking wood for campfires or grass to feed their animals may inadvertently strip the surrounding terrain. In Asia, deforestation has also compromised the habitat of Javan and Sumatran rhinos.

Population growth, nonsustainable agricultural policies, and rural poverty all force people to forage for fuel, leading to deforestation. Today fuelwood collection is a greater cause of deforestation in Asian tropical forests than logging. According to the Asian Development Bank (AsDB), communities living on the perimeter of the Asian-Pacific forests cut 700 million cubic meters of timber a year— seven times the amount lumber companies harvest annually. Between 1980 and 1990, the total forest area of the Asian-Pacific region was reduced by 9 percent, an average loss that was more than double the annual replanting rate. In response to these statistics, the Asian Development Bank outlined a plan to protect Asia's forests by encouraging sustainable harvesting and promoting pricing policies that encourage the use of energy alternatives to wood, such as biogas (a synthetic fuel), kerosene, and solar power. Richard Bradley, director of the AsDB agriculture department, said the bank's plan encouraged "intensive [agricultural] production on existing lowlands rather than farming by clearing forestlands. They will also promote tree-planting in upland areas under cultivation and reforestation on degraded forestlands."

In Nepal, a shortage of pasture land has driven people to graze their cattle in the country's national parks and reserves. By doing so, they take available food and habitat away from the rhinoceros population, and they put the wild rhinos at risk of contracting domestic cattle diseases. Nepalese villagers and squatters also cut trees in the parks for fire and fuelwood. To help solve the problem of cattle grazing and deforestation in Nepal's Royal Chitwan National Park, the warden ordered sections of grass to be grown around the perimeter of the park and cut daily for villagers to bring to their cattle. By keeping their cattle enclosed in pens, villagers could collect their dung and burn it for fuel. The warden also decided to have park workers collect dead trees from within the park and bring them outside to a collection point where villagers could obtain the wood. These solutions were approved by the Nepalese government in 1993.

Environmental conservation

The Nepalese solution, an example of the macroeconomic perspective on habitat management, allowed wildlife managers to gain the cooperation and participation of local people in their conservation strategy. Without incentives to help save rhinos, local people may look upon them as only a nuisance, since they are known for making nocturnal raids on farmers' crops. But by reinvesting rhino-related income back into local communities, villagers can be assured that saving the rhino is a worthy cause. For example, by placing a tax on hotel and tour operators—the main beneficiaries of rhino-related tourism—governments of the range states can use a portion of their tourism revenue to fund community development projects, helping to involve local people in the welfare of the rhinos. Habitat conservation strategies have increasingly come to rely on the involvement of local people to help protect the habitat of the rhinos.

In 1989 the World Wide Fund for Nature initiated a community forestry project among subsistence farmers living around Nepal's Royal Chitwan National Park. Thousands of native saplings were planted, along with thatch grass, in the buffer area between the park and residential settlements. The success of this community forest venture prompted the fund to create a larger project with the Nature Conservancy and the World Resources Institute that involves more than sixty thousand subsistence farmers living around

A reforestation worker looks after seedling pine trees in Nepal. The reforestation project provides fuel for farmers so they will not need to raid the rhino habitat for firewood.

the park. The project provides farmers with firewood and grass, restores degraded land, and plants forests in the buffer zone around the park. In this way, local people do not need to raid the park for their sustenance, and the rhino habitat is preserved. Programs aimed at conserving the habitat of rhinos and local people have also been initiated in Indonesia, where almost all lowland forests have been cleared for rice cultivation to feed a population as large as that of the United States but concentrated into only 10 percent of the land area.

There are ways to balance the needs of rhinoceroses and people. In India, where many people make their living by logging, compromises have been made between wildlife officials seeking to protect rhino forest habitat and the timber industry. A study conducted by the World Wildlife Fund in the early 1980s found that the Sumatran rhinoceros could live in areas that had been selectively logged, rather than clear-cut. In fact, selective logging actually helped the rhinos by allowing room for more food plants in the forest. The thinning of the forest, however, made it easier for poachers to track rhinoceroses, so patrols are now maintained in areas where the forest has been thinned.

As habitat encroachment shrinks rhino populations, consolidation may be the key to the rhinoceros's survival. Like all living things, rhinos become more vulnerable as their numbers decrease. Surviving rhinos face the pressures associated with small populations.

Loss of viability: the hazards of small populations

Rhinos are threatened because they have been reduced, in many areas, to marginal populations that face pressures large populations are capable of withstanding. Small populations are vulnerable to genetic, environmental, and demographic problems. Loss of genetic diversity is a problem faced by dwindling populations in the wild as well as small captive ones. As the rhino's habitat is fragmented and populations become smaller and cut off from one another, rhinos may end up mating with relatives, limiting the genetic diversity essential for any species to adapt to changing environments; on the individual level, genetic diversity is important for the development of healthy, viable offspring. At least some members of a genetically diverse population, for example, would be able to survive the introduction of a new disease. As the number of potential genetic partnerships shrinks with the demise of rhino populations, the gene pool is converted to a "gene puddle" that offers less diversity and threatens the survival of rhinos. Small populations lead to increased inbreeding, which causes lower survival rates and reduced population growth.

Shrinking populations are also vulnerable to demographic problems such as uneven sex ratios. Many surviving rhino populations consist of fewer than one hundred breeding individuals, insufficient to weather chance events such as too few females being born or natural disasters that can reduce the number of breeding males and females. Captive breeding programs in American zoos have tried to deal with the problem of uneven sex ratios by transporting male rhinos from zoo to zoo to breed with cows. However, these attempts are not always successful, as introduced animals will not always mate. In the wild, uneven sex ratios lead to a species' demise. Other demographic problems occur when reproduction cannot keep up with mortality rates or when age gradients within a population are too distorted. If there are young bulls but no young cows in a population, for example, the only females available for the males to mate with may be too old to raise new cows before they die.

Environmental hazards such as epidemics or natural disasters can also devastate small populations. Five Javan rhinos died of a virus in Indonesia's Ujong Kulon National Park, causing park officials to worry that inbreeding had reduced the Javan rhino's genetic variability. Conservationists have tried to determine the minimum viable population necessary to survive potential genetic, demographic, and environmental problems. Given the slow rate of reproduction among rhinos, a large population is essential to survival. Preliminary studies indicate that each species of rhinoceros requires at least five hundred individuals to be considered a stable population.

Increasing carrying capacity

If available rhino habitat continues to shrink, more rhinos will be concentrated into smaller reserves, where wildlife officials will face the challenge of managing as many rhinos as possible in a reduced area. To increase the carrying capacity of the land—the population that an area can successfully support—scientists are now investigating the behavioral patterns of rhinos. Since they are accustomed to roaming alone over large areas, rhinos are somewhat antisocial and not used to tolerating the presence of other rhinos in their feeding areas. They often act aggressively toward one another when populations become too dense. However, zoologists believe that rhinos may grow accustomed to living in proximity with other rhinos and modify their aggressive behavior, much in the way black rhinos that were in frequent contact with humans ceased to act aggressively toward them. Zoologists hope rhinos will be able to form tolerant social groups, thus allowing conservationists to accommodate and protect larger groups within smaller areas.

Translocation

To ensure their long-term survival, wildlife managers relocate rhinoceros populations to IPZs and private sanctuaries. After the failure of Operation Stronghold in the late 1980s, Zimbabwe began a translocation program to remove rhinos from the Zambezi Valley, where rampant poaching was difficult to control. Rhinos were first tracked by scouts, then darted with tranquilizers from a helicopter. The drugged animals were crated and transported to specially protected reserves and heavily guarded private sanctuaries working in conjunction with the government. So far, Zimbabwe's translocation program has succeeded in protecting its rhinos.

At three thousand pounds, this white rhinoceros bull is still five hundred pounds underweight due to a two-year drought in the area. Game park workers are preparing the rhino for translocation to a nearby farm as part of a wildlife relocation program.

Translocating small, scattered rhino populations to a few relatively large sanctuaries where protection efforts can be concentrated more effectively has worked to save rhinos, and sanctuaries consistently prove to be the safest places for wild rhino populations. Often privately owned and heavily guarded, sanctuaries are surrounded by electric fences to keep poachers out, and they are better equipped to win the war against poachers than the often poorly funded government programs in the developing countries where rhinos range. International conservation organizations have collaborated with governments in some of the range states to create effective sanctuaries. In Kenya, for example, the World Wildlife Fund provided funding for an electric fence surrounding the country's first government-operated rhino sanctuary at Lake Nakuru National Park, where the black rhino population has since grown. Individuals in Kenya have also collaborated with the state to create a model of wildlife conservation. By constructing sanctuaries on private land, some citizens have assumed the financial responsibility for ownership and operation of rhino sanctuaries.

Expenses

Sanctuaries are a costly solution to rhino conservation, however, frequently costing over $1 million to develop and over $100,000 per year to operate. One private sanctuary in Zimbabwe spends nearly $3,500 per year on each rhino. Many privately funded sanctuaries raise revenue by hosting tourists and photo safaris. The South African government annually rounds up around one hundred of its rhinos and sells them to sanctuaries and game lodges that will protect and care for the animals in the hope of attracting tourists. Money from the government sale of rhinos helps the state in its own conservation efforts. In 1992 the Natal Parks Board sold five black rhinos for close to $800,000. According to the board, those who buy the rhinos are better able to protect them than the government: "A guy who's paid 2 million rand [$800,000] for five rhino has a stock in them and he's going to look after them."

In 1997, the IUCN released a report concluding that the private sector has played an invaluable role in the conservation of wildlife in Africa. In contrast with socialist countries that do not allow the holding of private property, African countries with free market economies have been successful in getting private individuals and companies to invest in conservation-oriented enterprises. Noting the significant role that private sanctuaries have played in wildlife conservation, the IUCN urges that economic incentives be offered to encourage individuals to keep private land under wildlife management. Kenya has fifty such privately protected areas, some of which promote ecotourism as a means of gathering revenue and making sustainable use of wildlife.

Ecotourism

The rhino conservation movement has begun to consider the fund-raising potential of ecotourism ventures, as well as their ability to educate the public about conservation. Ecotourism is a type of travel that introduces visitors to the culture, terrain, and wildlife of a country without impacting the host environment. Ecotourist facilities are constructed in keeping with the culture and lifestyles of the host country, and they attempt to provide tourists with a realistic experience of life in the country. In 1997 the International Rhino Foundation invested in an ecotourism facility in conjunction with the Sumatran Rhino Sanctuary at Way Kambas National Park in Indonesia. This ecotourism program, which exposes visitors to the habitat and lifestyle of Sumatran rhinos, is expected to generate significant income for Sumatran rhino conservation in Indonesia within three to four years, while helping to educate the public about the pressures the rhinoceros faces.

Ecotourism offers numerous benefits to wildlife populations and habitats, local people, tourists, and the economies of developing countries. Bringing tourists into a country introduces them to another culture and environment, helping to enhance cross-cultural understanding and spread awareness about the country's environment and natural resources. By emphasizing low-impact travel, ecotourism claims not to significantly change the culture of the host country. In addition, the money from tourism benefits local merchants and service providers, and user fees can funnel tourist revenue into local agricultural, forestry, and water projects. Thus, ecotourism provides an economic incentive to stop poaching and to protect wildlife habitats. In 1990 over $200 billion was spent on ecotourism activities, and the World Tourism Organization predicts that ecotourism, currently the fastest growing sector of the tourism industry, will continue to grow.

'It's a herd of wildlife camera crews.'

Conservationists can point to some success stories in their quest to preserve the rhino's habitat. Through the efforts of individuals, organizations, and governments to set aside land for rhinos, the black rhino population of Namibia increased from three hundred in 1980 to five hundred by 1992. In South Africa the southern white rhino population continues to expand after being translocated and reestablished on private land. Current growth rates of 6 to 8 percent per year indicate that the southern white rhino population could double from seven thousand to fourteen thousand within ten years if the habitat available to them continues to expand. And from the early 1960s to the 1990s, the number of Indian rhinos in Nepal rose from eighty to over four hundred. Nevertheless, the world rhinoceros population continues to be fewer than eleven thousand. The future of the rhino is still uncertain.

5

The Future of
the Rhino

THE DRASTIC DECLINE in African and Asian rhino populations has led wildlife organizations like the WWF to assess the effectiveness of their approach to rhino conservation and to conduct cost-benefit analyses. Intervening before a species is critically endangered is much more cost effective than launching a recovery operation, but since Asian rhinoceroses, especially Javan and Sumatran rhinos, are now seriously endangered, the cost of their recovery over the next five years is estimated at $60 to $100 million. Even more than that will be necessary to save Africa's rhino population. Mollie Beattie, director of the U.S. Fish and Wildlife Service, notes that "Recovery is like emergency room medicine. It costs more than seeing your regular doctor for preventative care. And it costs more to recover endangered species than it would have cost to prevent their decline in the first place." Money spent to save rhinos and their habitat, however, would have side benefits for all of the other animals and plants that share that habitat. Thus, rhinos serve as the poster animals for their habitat.

The public appeal of an endangered species may affect the priority it is assigned. Seventy percent of endangered species represented by the Species Survival Project (SSP), a global network that oversees the breeding of endangered species in American zoos, are mammals—primarily large, exotic species that have captured widespread public support.

The cost of recovery for the Javan and Sumatran rhinos is estimated at $60 to $100 million over the next five years. Recovering Africa's rhino population will be even more expensive.

It is no accident that the World Wide Fund for Nature chose the giant panda, a cuddly-looking creature, for its logo; it is easier to arouse public sympathy for a panda than for the more abstract idea of an ecosystem. Today the panda is arguably one of the most popular and recognizable endangered animals. Although it presents a harsher exterior to the world, the rhino is also a large, charismatic animal that has attracted a conservation following. But since the most popular endangered species are not necessarily the ones whose roles in nature are most vital, a species-specific conservation movement may not be the most efficient. Yale professor Steven R. Bessinger advocates a focus on the preservation of whole ecosystems. "Instead of taking a species-by-species crisis approach to conservation, we should focus on preserving the ecosystems that support a wide variety of plants and animals."

Maintaining biodiversity

One of the major reasons cited for why rhinos should be saved is the cause of biodiversity. Indeed, biodiversity is listed as an important reason for the preservation of any endangered species. Biological diversity, the multitude of different living organisms on the earth, is essential to the healthy functioning of ecosystems. Scientists are still uncertain about the magnitude of effects the extinction of any one species can have on an entire ecosystem, but evidence suggests the potential for ripple effects. One devastating example occurred on Borneo in the 1950s when the island was sprayed with DDT, a powerful insecticide, to wipe out malaria-spreading mosquitoes. Mosquitoes died from the DDT, but then lizards, who feed on insects, ate the dead mosquitoes. Cats then ate the lizards, causing them to die of DDT poisoning. The widespread disappearance of cats on the island led to a proliferation of rats. Rats, which are carriers of disease, then brought a plague epidemic to the island. The situation grew desperate, and eventually a fresh supply of cats had to be brought to Borneo to kill off the rats and stem the plague. Since each part of an ecosystem is linked to other parts in a web of interrelationships, the loss of a species affects the entire ecosystem. Recognizing the importance of biodiversity to all life forms, the United Nations held the Convention on Biological Diversity at the Rio Earth Summit in 1992. Endorsed by 157 countries, the convention stressed that biological diversity is one of the earth's greatest assets "for supporting economic development and for maintaining human welfare all over the world."

When it is too late to save a habitat itself, or when a species is so critically threatened that it has no other options, conservationists resort to a stopgap measure known as captive breeding to keep a species alive. The Sumatran rhino has become part of captive breeding experiments.

Captive breeding

Captive breeding involves capturing animals and moving them from unprotected areas in the wild to breeding facilities in captivity. These facilities are designed to keep the species from becoming extinct while protected areas are being established, and only species that are on the brink of extinction are selected for this conservation strategy. Since species bred in captivity can increase faster than is possible in the wild, the goal of captive breeding programs is to replace depleted stock and reestablish wild populations.

The SSP works with captive breeding programs to ensure that genetic diversity is maintained and that inbreeding does not occur. Each breeding facility keeps careful records to ensure biological diversity, and animals are transferred between facilities on breeding loans to accomplish this goal. Genetic research on rhinos is currently underway at a number of universities in the hope that results will help preserve the genetic integrity and diversity of rhinos that live in captive breeding centers. In addition, by studying captive rhinos and learning more about their reproduction, zoologists work to make breeding programs more effective.

A failed attempt

Because their habitat has been so devastated by commercial development, Sumatran rhinos were selected for a captive breeding program known as the Sumatran Rhino Trust, a partnership between American and Indonesian zoos begun in 1985. Four North American zoos—the Cincinnati Zoo, the Los Angeles Zoo, the San Diego Zoo, and the Bronx Zoo—worked with the Indonesian government to establish this program, in which Sumatran rhinos were captured in the wild and sent to captive breeding centers at zoos in Indonesia and America.

But eight years and millions of dollars later, the program had failed to produce a single offspring. Of the thirty-nine rhinos captured for the project, twenty-one died. The reasons for the high mortality rate and lack of reproduction are still unknown. It is suspected that the rhinos might require larger enclosures and more natural conditions than were provided for them in captivity. Lacking any positive result, the initiative was abandoned.

According to Thomas Foose, program officer for the International Rhino Foundation, a new plan has been announced to breed Sumatran rhinos in Indonesian sanctuaries rather than in zoos abroad, with the hope that this will provide more natural living conditions for the rhinos in their native habitat. For example, males and females are normally separate in the wild, except when females are in estrus, and this situation will be mirrored in the new Indonesian facility. The IRF is helping to fund the construction of this facility at Way Kambas National Park, which will have a breeding center, natural enclosures, and an ecotourist lodge.

A collaboration between the American Zookeepers' Association and the Species Survival Project has produced a recent baby boom among SSP captive rhino populations in the United States. Since 1995 the partnership has recorded thirty-two new rhino births and only three fatalities. Nineteen of the new calves were black rhinos; the remainder

A one-week-old Indian rhinoceros calf stays close to its mother at the Zoological Gardens in Philadelphia, Pennsylvania.

were southern white rhinos and Indian rhinos. The efficacy of captive breeding, however, continues to be the subject of much debate.

The argument against captive breeding

Captive breeding is a controversial issue. Zoo officials and wildlife experts from the National Zoo, Yale University, and the San Diego Wild Animal Park have argued that captive breeding, which should be viewed as a last resort for endangered species, is being used as part of a long-term conservation strategy. "Captive breeding is no panacea for saving endangered species," warns Steven R. Bessinger, Yale professor of ecology and conservation biology. "In some cases, captive breeding has meant the difference between survival and extinction. By no means are we saying it shouldn't be used in those cases, but captive breeding is being proposed with increasing frequency when it's not appropriate." Critics cite the increased allocation of funds for captive breeding programs, despite what have proven to be serious limitations, such as high costs, the threat of disease, and a general lack of success in returning animals to

This two-day-old, seventy-two-pound rhinoceros was born in captivity to a four-thousand-pound rhino named Lulu at the Metro Zoo in Miami, Florida. Some critics of captive breeding programs believe conservationists should focus their efforts on protecting the remaining rhinos that live in the wild.

the wild. Although captive breeding programs have made tremendous advances with in vitro fertilization techniques and genetic management, critics argue that the long-term future of endangered species lies in their ability to exist in the wild, and they believe that efforts should be focused on securing their habitat and making it possible for the animals to exist in the wild.

Critics of captive breeding programs fear that the existence of captive populations will give an erroneous impression that a species is safe, making the need to protect its habitat in the wild less urgent. "The false sense of buying time that captive breeding creates can undermine the sense of urgency about fixing the environmental problems that threaten species in the first place," maintains Noel Snyder of the Wildlife Preservation Trust. Professor Bessinger concurs that "More attention should be focused on correcting conditions in the wild that are threatening species survival." Unless the conditions that initially led to a species' endangerment are corrected, reintroducing captive-bred species into the wild is bound to be ineffective.

Currently 70 percent of all recovery plans for endangered species include captive breeding programs, which annually cost an estimated $250,000 to $500,000 per species. Another drawback to captive breeding is that animals in captivity can become domesticated in less than two generations, making it impossible for them to be reintroduced successfully into the wild. "Evolution does not stop just because species are in cages," explains Scott Derrickson of the National Zoo. "Essential behavioral traits are especially prone to rapid loss in captivity, making it less likely that the animals will be successfully reintroduced to the wild."

Reintroduction of captive-bred species

Although there is not yet enough evidence to determine whether rhinos born in captivity can be successfully released, at least one rhino has made the transition. In September 1996 the Serengeti Park Zoo in Hoden Hagen, Germany, released the first captive-born white rhino into the wild. Born in Germany, Kay, a five-year-old male white

rhino, was successfully released into Namibia's Etosha
National Park, where, after a period of transition, he was
able to achieve his zoo's goal by joining a wild white rhino
population.

Some captive breeding programs, such as that for the
black-footed ferret, have succeeded in reintroducing captive-
bred species into the wild. Although the initial mortality
rate among reintroduced ferrets was high, researchers estimate that by releasing 40 to 50 captive-bred ferrets per
year, the population will be self-sustaining within five
years. However, only 11 percent of 145 different captive
breeding programs have been successful in reintroducing
species into the wild. In the unsuccessful cases, captive-
bred animals lacked essential survival skills such as the
know-how to find food, escape predators, and migrate to
breeding grounds. And even when captive-bred species are
successfully reintroduced into protected habitats, they
sometimes bring with them new diseases, acquired through
contact with other species at the zoo, and infect native populations. Although isolating captive species from permanent zoo animals and conducting medical screenings
before reintroduction might reduce the spread of disease,
most zoos do not have sufficient space or money to provide
separate housing within a species.

The role of zoos in rhinoceros conservation

There are currently about one thousand rhinos in captivity around the world. Some of these rhinos are permanently
housed in zoos, while others are part of captive breeding
programs whose ultimate goal is to return the animals to
the wild. Since over 116 million people visit North America's 165 zoos each year, zoos have the potential to educate
significant numbers of people about rhino conservation.
According to a study in *Conservation Biology*, zoos have a
tremendous potential to promote biological diversity and
to help endangered species through public education.
However, zoos also have many limitations to overcome.
According to David Hancocks, director of the Arizona-
Sonora Desert Museum, the future of the industry lies in

changing the structure of zoos so they can educate visitors about entire ecosystems. Currently, Hancocks notes, zoos are not emphasizing the connections between species:

> [Zoos] do not exhibit and interpret the complexity of habitats. . . . Typically, zoos are arranged taxonomically, i.e., visitors go to one place to see bears, then another to see monkeys, or birds, or reptiles, and so on. In addition, almost every zoo duplicates the same collection, focusing principally on mammalian, diurnal, African, cute, pretty, social and essentially charismatic large species. . . . Zoos cannot present the connections between soils, plants, and animals.

This three-month-old white rhinoceros is one of about one thousand rhinos in captivity.

By using their collections to educate the public about the interrelationships of nature and by sharing their revenue with research and conservation efforts in the wild, zoos can make great strides to protect rhinos and all endangered species.

Many zoos now funnel part of their revenue to rhino conservation projects within the countries where rhinos make their home. The Minnesota Zoo, for example, participates in the Adopt-a-Park program, in which it sends donations directly to Ujong Kulon National Park to support the Javan rhino conservation project. And the Cincinnati Zoo, which participated in the Sumatran Rhino Trust experiment, is now focusing on educating the public about the need for habitat preservation. Zoo director Edward Maruska comments on the future of zoos:

> While captive breeding for future reintroduction will continue to be an important part of zoo conservation efforts, our objective in captive breeding should not be to have a lot of frozen animals in straws or living museum pieces with no habitat to place them in. A more critical role that we will continue to play is in environmental education. Educating our public about the necessity and urgency of preserving valuable habitat is essential to the survival of endangered species. Our main efforts should be focused on ways to protect habitat worldwide and on using our captive breeding efforts and technology to shore up endangered populations of existing species.

To promote the conservation of rhinos, many zoos now donate part of their profits to rhino conservation projects, such as the Adopt-a-Park program and the Sumatran Rhino Trust experiment.

Saving rhinos

Throughout history, humans have been interested in the rhinoceros. Stone Age peoples drew pictures of rhinoceroses on cave walls. Twenty-five-hundred-year-old cups

carved from rhino horn have been found in ancient Persia. Ancient Romans put a live rhinoceros on display. Marco Polo saw a rhino in Sumatra and thought surely that it was a unicorn. Perhaps the uniqueness of these creatures and the fact that they are so very different from us is what has attracted human beings to rhinoceroses.

"One of the great tragedies of the 21st century will be humanity's homogeneity," laments Nan Schaffer, founder of SOS Rhino and the Rhino Reproduction Program in Chicago.

> Everywhere, everything will be the same. That which we could not tame or imitate will be gone. No matter how hard we try, we cannot "build" nature. We can build another bridge, paint another picture, but we cannot make another rhino. Look into a really wild animal's eyes. When the wild things are gone, we will lose our place, our way; for whose eyes will we look into to find our humility, our humanity?

Conservation organizations are working to help save endangered plant and animal life now so future generations will be able to experience this same awe and wonder toward the rhinoceros, and all of the earth's biodiversity. Many individuals, organizations, and government bodies are involved in the effort to protect rhinos, and though they share the same goal of saving rhinos, each person's commitment to preserving this species may differ. As one park guard in Africa exclaimed, "My heart says the fact that we have rhinos is reason enough to look after them."

Glossary

alpha males: The dominant, most successful males; alpha rhinos often maintain their own feeding and breeding territories, which they defend against other males.

artiodactyl: An ungulate with an even number of toes, such as camels, deer, and pigs.

bull: A male rhinoceros.

CITES: (Convention on International Trade in Endangered Species) An international treaty to ban the trade in endangered animals and their products, signed by 130 countries and dating from 1977.

cow: A female rhinoceros.

dehorning: An initiative undertaken by wildlife conservationists in some countries to remove the horns of rhinos in the hope of devaluing the animals to poachers.

djambia: A ceremonial dagger worn by men in Yemen; the handle is sometimes made from rhinoceros horn.

ecotourism: An industry that promotes conservation efforts by generating jobs and money for local economies while spreading environmental awareness through a low-impact approach on the host environment and culture.

estrus: The cyclic period during which a female rhino is able to become pregnant.

keratin: The same substance that forms human fingernails; on rhinos, keratin forms long hairlike fibers that fuse into a solid horn.

pachyderm: A mammal with thick skin, such as an elephant, hippopotamus, or rhinoceros.

perissodactyl: An ungulate with an odd number of toes, such as the rhino and the horse.

poaching: The illegal killing of an animal for some part of its body, i.e., hide, horns, and tusks.

prehensile: That which is adapted for seizing or grasping.

sanctuaries: Heavily guarded refuges for wildlife where predators are controlled and hunting is illegal; often privately owned.

subsidiary males: Male rhinos who are younger or less successful than alpha males and thus not in control of territory.

translocation: The practice of transporting wild rhinos from unsafe, high poaching areas to more heavily guarded reserves and private sanctuaries.

ungulates: An ancient family of mammals that were the first to develop hooves.

Organizations
to Contact

African Wildlife Update
4739 Fox Trail Dr. NE
Olympia, WA 98516
(360) 459-8862
fax: (360) 459-8771
Internet: http://www.africanwildlife.org

African Wildlife Update is a bimonthly newsletter published by the African Wildlife News Service and is available by subscription. The site also features on-line exclusives.

Environmental Investigation Agency (EIA)
1611 Connecticut Ave. NW, Suite 3B
Washington, DC 20009
(202) 483-6621
fax: (202) 483-6625
e-mail: eiauk@gn.apc.org

The EIA spearheads international efforts to protect endangered species, including rhinos, tigers, bears, elephants, whales, dolphins, porpoises, and wild birds.

Friends of Conservation (FOC)
1520 Kensington Rd., Suite 201
Oak Brook, IL 60521
(708) 954-3388
fax: (708) 954-1016

FOC is committed to promoting a balance between the needs of local peoples in Kenya's Masai Mara game reserve and the needs of the reserve's wildlife. FOC also monitors the black rhino and educates primary and secondary school students about conservation and the value of wildlife to the community's well-being.

International Rhino Foundation (IRF)

14000 International Rd.
Cumberland, OH 43732
Internet: http://www. rhinos-irf.org

The International Rhino Foundation is a conservation organization dedicated to helping rhinoceroses. The IRF funds programs and research worldwide to help the most threatened rhino species and is currently collaborating with Indonesia to create a Sumatran rhino breeding facility and ecotourism site in Sumatra.

The Rhino Trust

4045 N. Massachusetts
Portland, OR 97227
(503) 288-3521
fax: (503) 287-5087

The Rhino Trust supports efforts to protect the world's five rhinoceros species within their native habitats through fundraising, public awareness, and education.

SOS Rhino

Internet: http://www.sosrhino.org

SOS Rhino works to heighten awareness of the plight of the rhinoceros. It is funded by the Milwaukee County Zoo as part of the Rhinoceros Reproduction Program, founded in 1983 by Nan Schaffer, to breed rhinos in captivity. In addition to fund-raising, research, and conservation, SOS Rhino works to focus worldwide attention on the threats facing rhinos.

Species Survival Commission

Internet: http://www.iucn.org/themes/ssc/index.html

The mission of the Species Survival Commission, a volunteer commission of the IUCN, is to conserve biological diversity by developing and executing programs to study, save, restore, and manage species and their habitats.

U.S. Fish and Wildlife Service
Endangered Species and Habitat Conservation
400 Arlington Sq.
18th and C Streets NW
Washington, DC 20240
(703) 358-2171

The U.S. Fish and Wildlife Service funds conservation programs in American schools and communities and is currently working to educate U.S. citizens about the threats rhinos face from the demand for rhino horn medications.

World Wildlife Fund (WWF)
1250 24th St. NW
PO Box 96555
Washington, DC 20077-7795
(800) CALL WWF
Internet: http://www.wwf.org

The WWF was founded in 1961 and leads worldwide efforts to protect threatened wildlife and habitats. International in scope, the WWF network is positioned to act quickly when conservation emergencies arise. Since 1961 the WWF has channeled over $13 million into rhino-related conservation projects in Asia and Africa. It also researches and monitors the rhino horn trade.

Suggestions for Further Reading

Caroline Arnold and Richard Hewett, *Rhino*. New York: Morrow Junior Books, 1995. Beautifully photographed story of the lives of rhinos in captivity.

Amanda Harman, *Rhinoceroses*. New York: Benchmark Books, 1997. Informative overview of the five types of rhinoceroses and the ways in which they are threatened.

Thane Maynard, *A Rhino Comes to America*. New York: Franklin Watts, 1993. Written by the director of the Cincinnati Zoo, this book offers an informative discussion of rhinos and the effort to breed Sumatran rhinos in captivity in the United States.

Sally M. Walker, *Rhinos*. Minneapolis: Carolrhoda Books, 1996. Well-photographed book that discusses the lifestyle and social organization of rhinos.

Works Consulted

Joel Berger, "Science, Conservation, and Black Rhinos," *Journal of Mammalogy* 75 (2): 298–308m, 1994. A study of dehorning programs for black and white rhinoceroses in Africa and their implications for conservation.

Kenneth Brower, "Devouring the Earth," *Atlantic Monthly*, November 1994, pp. 113–26. Discussion of the trade in endangered wildlife products with emphasis on work being done to detect underground trade networks.

Camia Catalina, "Panel Moves to Stem Poaching of Rhinos and Tigers," *Congressional Quarterly*, August 13, 1994, p. 2334. Analysis of the House Merchant Marine and Fisheries Committee testimony of August 1994.

Sara Chamberlain, "Armed Rebellion Imperils Indian Rhinos," *Earth Island Journal*, Winter 1995, p. 17. How rhinoceros horn, because of its value, is being taken to fund arms for rebel movements.

Jean Clottes, "Rhinos and Lions and Bears," *Natural History*, May 1995, pp. 30–36. Discovery of cave paintings of rhinos in France, made during the Paleolithic era.

Carol Cunningham and Joel Berger, "The De-Horning Dilemma," *Wildlife Conservation*, January/February 1994, p. 15. Discusses how dehorning initiatives have adversely affected black rhino populations in Africa.

Carol Cunningham and Joel Berger, "Horns, Hyenas, and Black Rhinos," *Research and Exploration*, Spring 1994, pp. 241–44. Explains how dehorning female rhinos affects calf mortality.

D. C. Denison, "Interview with Michael Werikhe," *Boston Globe Magazine*, August 18, 1991. An interview with a Kenyan rhino conservationist and activist.

"Fumbi, Under Guard," *Economist*, March 5, 1994, p. 50. The increasing role of private sanctuaries in the rhino conservation movement.

Nick Haslam, "The Rhinos of Kaziranga," *Financial Times*, September 21–22, 1996, p. 5. Antipoaching patrols in Kaziranga, Assam, to protect Indian rhinoceroses.

Peter Y. Hong, "Remedy to Extinction," *Los Angeles Times*, October 20, 1995, p. B 3:2. A U.S. campaign to deter consumers from medicinal wildlife products.

Sam LaBudde, "Rhinos-to-Go: Speculating on Extinction," *Earth Island Journal*, Winter 1995, p. 17. Discusses how rhino extinction would affect the sale and value of rhinoceros products.

Les Line, "Genetic Differences in Rhinos Complicate Conservation Effort," *New York Times*, January 14, 1997. A debate over whether captive breeding programs should maintain the genetic diversity of the Sumatran rhinos.

Esmond Bradley Martin, *Rhino Exploitation*. Hong Kong: World Wildlife Fund, 1983. Covers the medicinal uses of rhinoceros parts around the world.

"New Commission Builds on Earth Summit Legacy," *UN Chronicle*, September 1993, p. 62. Role of UN Environment Program (UNEP) in rhinoceros protection.

Malcolm Penny, *Rhinos: Endangered Species*. New York: Facts On File, 1988. Informative account of the five types of rhinoceroses and their evolutionary history, as well as an overview of the problems rhinoceroses face today.

Dieter and Mary Plage, "Return of Java's Wildlife," *National Geographic*, June 1985, p. 760. The Javan rhinos of Ujong Kulon.

Alan R. Rabinowitz, "On the Horns of a Dilemma," *Wildlife Conservation*, September/October 1994, pp. 34–39. Plight of the Sumatran rhinoceros.

Donna Rosenthal, "Showdown in Zimbabwe," *International Wildlife*, November/December 1996, pp. 28–35. How Zimbabwe has used antiguerilla warfare, translocation programs, and community education to crack down on poaching.

Liz Sly, "Unknown Enemy," *Chicago Tribune*, November 8, 1994, section 7, 5:1. Bizarre incident of rhino killings by African elephants.

Timothy M. Swanson, "The Economics of Extinction Revisited and Revised: A Generalized Framework for the Analysis of the Problems of Endangered Species and Biodiversity Losses," *Oxford Economic Papers*, October 1994, pp. 800–820. Explains how policies regarding endangered animals must be shaped to address the fundamental forces behind extinction.

"Two Rare White Rhinos Die in Transit in China," *New York Times*, December 17, 1996, p. A5. Neglect and ineptitude cause the deaths of two white rhinos given to the Chinese by the San Diego Zoo.

U.S. House Committee on Science and Technology, Subcommittee on Natural Resources, Agriculture Research, and Environment, *Hearings on Conservation of the Endangered Rhinoceros*. Washington, DC: GPO, June 22, 1988.

Christopher Wren, "Walking with Rhinoceroses," *New York Times*, February 21, 1993, p. 114. Rhino-related tourism and conservation in South Africa.

On-line Sources

Mark Atkinson, "Dehorning," March 26, 1997, International Rhino Foundation website, http://www.rhino-irf.org.

Mark Atkinson, "International Rhino Foundation Sponsored Programs and Research," March 26, 1997, International Rhino Foundation website, http://www.rhino-irf.org.

Kate Burling, "Captive-Born White Rhino Released into Namibia's Etosha National Park," September 1996, African Wildlife Update website, http://www.africanwildlife.org.

Kate Burling, "Poachers Kill Two of Garamba's Rare Northern White Rhinos," April 1, 1996, African Wildlife Update website, http://www.africanwildlife.org.

David Hancocks, "Can Zoos Survive?" *Animals International*, Summer 1995. Available from http://www.way.net/wspa/wscnzoo.html.

International Union for Conservation of Nature, "Analyses of Proposals to Amend the CITES Appendices," June 6, 1997, reference document 10.89, no. 10.28, IUCN website, http://www.iucn.org.

InterPress Service, "Regional Bank Unveils New Forestry Policy," March 6, 1995, InterPress Service website, http://www.lanic.utexas.edu/la/region/news/arec/lasnet/1995/0493.html.

Julie A. Kreiner, "Interview with Nan Schaffer," March 27, 1997, SOS Rhino website, http://www.sosrhino.org. An interview with the founder of SOS Rhino and the Rhino Reproduction Program.

Claude Martin, "Rhinos in the Wild: Saving 60 Million Years of Evolution," March 27, 1997, World Wildlife Fund website, http://www.wwf.org. Executive summary of the

WWF's rhinoceros conservation efforts, written by the organization's director general.

Claude Martin, "WWF, the Rhino, and the Facts of Death," May 1997, World Wildlife Fund website, http://www.wwf.org.

Edward Maruska, "Captive Breeding: Is It the Answer?" June 11, 1997, Cincinnati Zoo website, http://www.cincyzoo.org.

"Nature Body Says Zaire Wildlife Threatened by War," January 27, 1997, SOS Rhino website, Rhino News page, http://www.sosrhino.org.

Marcela Rabi, "Black Rhino Trade," Fall 1996. Available from http://www.gurukul.ucc.american.edu.

"Rhinos," January 22, 1997, SOS Rhino website, Rhino News page, http://www.sosrhino.org.

Yale University, "Captive Breeding No Panacea for Endangered Species," June 14, 1996, News Wise website, http://www.newswise.com.

Index

Picture Credits

About the Author

Mary Hull was twenty years old when she saw her first rhinoceros, a *Diceros bicornis*, at Ngorongoro Crater in Tanzania. She hopes to return to East Africa in the near future. In 1997 Ms. Hull's book *Struggle and Love* was recognized by the New York Public Library Association as one of the best books of the year for teenagers.